SAT

FOR

DUMMIES

A Wiley Brand

Quick Prep Edition

*SAT FOR DUMMIES
A Wiley Brand

Quick Prep Edition

by Geraldine Woods and Ron Woldoff

FOR DUMMIES
A Wiley Brand

*SAT For Dummies®, Quick Prep Edition

Published by
John Wiley & Sons, Inc.,
111 River Street
Hoboken, NJ 07030-5774
www.wiley.com

Copyright © 2015 by John Wiley & Sons, Inc., Hoboken, New Jersey

Published simultaneously in Canada

For general information on our other products and services, please contact our Customer Care Department within the U.S. at 877-762-2974, outside the U.S. at 317-572-3993, or fax 317-572-4002.

For technical support, please visit www.wiley.com/techsupport.

Wiley publishes in a variety of print and electronic formats and by print-on-demand. Some material included with standard print versions of this book may not be included in e-books or in print-on-demand. If this book refers to media such as a CD or DVD that is not included in the version you purchased, you may download this material at http://booksupport.wiley.com. For more information about Wiley products, visit www.wiley.com.

Library of Congress Control Number: 2014954675

ISBN: 978-1-118-91157-0

ISBN 978-1-118-91157-0 (pbk); ISBN 978-1-118-91141-9 (ebk); ISBN 978-1-118-91172-3 (ebk)

Manufactured in the United States of America

10 9 8 7 6 5 4 3 2 1

Contents at a Glance

Table of Contents

Introduction

Change is good, right? So why do so many people hop on the nervous-breakdown train when they hear that the SAT is changing? Perhaps because the SAT is an important step on your journey to college, and anything to do with the admissions process is enough to give applicants an instant panic attack. Nervous or not, you have to take the SAT when you apply to most colleges or universities in the United States and to some English-speaking institutions abroad. The "old" SAT has been around since 2005 and was actually a redesign of a still older exam. The "new" SAT appears in March 2016. Because it's new, that version of the SAT may seem extra scary.

You have nothing to worry about, though, because you've been preparing for this version of the SAT for many years. What? You say you haven't been memorizing vocabulary words and drilling key math concepts since you were in your crib? How neglectful of you! Actually, you *have* been getting ready for the redesigned SAT, because you've been studying the necessary material during every single minute you devote to schoolwork, not counting lunch and the time you spend texting your friends from the phone hidden behind your science book. But those small lapses don't count for much when you consider the amount of time you've been analyzing and uncovering meaning when you read, organizing your ideas and writing papers, and solving math problems (more than 10,000 hours between kindergarten and tenth grade, according to a recent survey).

All those skills come in handy on the new SAT. The final step in preparing for the exam is the one you're taking now. You're reading this book and therefore becoming acquainted with the format of the test. By the time you're finished with *SAT For Dummies,* Quick Prep Edition, you'll have every possible tool for conquering the 2016 SAT.

Why change at all? The old SAT was loudly criticized for several reasons. It was long, hard, and tricky. Most important, it didn't accurately predict college success, its stated purpose. The College Board, which creates and administers the SAT, heard the complaints and hit the drawing board. What they came up with is still long and relatively hard, but the test more closely resembles the stuff you actually do in school. The reading and writing passages come from history, science, literary, and career-oriented sources. Some math questions draw on real-world situations. The new SAT also tests your ability to understand information presented visually, often in graphs or charts, and to recognize and evaluate evidence. The 2016 SAT eliminates some of its old tricks, such as the penalty for guessing, and lets you decide whether you want to write the essay. Add everything up, and you arrive at a test that concentrates on the skills you need to succeed in college and the workplace. (For details on the changes, check out Chapter 1.)

About This Book

SAT For Dummies, Quick Prep Edition, is a whirlwind tour of the redesigned SAT. (If you expect to take the old SAT at some point before the spring of 2016, turn to *SAT For Dummies,* 8th Edition, by Geraldine Woods, also published by Wiley.) This book takes you through each section of the 2016 SAT, explaining what the test-makers are looking for and how you can deliver it. For example, the new SAT makes a point of testing vocabulary in context, and that's how vocabulary shows up in *SAT For Dummies,* Quick Prep Edition. As you read, keep an eye out for words and definitions, including in paragraphs that have nothing to do with vocabulary *per se.* (By the way, **per se** means "as such" or "for itself.")

To help you step up your game on the SAT, this book includes in-depth analysis and samples of each type of question that the SAT dumps on you — reading comprehension, math grid-ins, and so forth. To kill still more of your free time (and help you improve your SAT-tested skills), you get a detailed explanation with each answer so you know what you answered correctly, what you got wrong, and why. To give you a feel for how ready you are to take the new SAT, try your hand at the practice test. No, it's not a real SAT because the company that produces the actual test is sitting on those rights. The test you get on test day may not have exactly the same number of questions in exactly the same order as the ones here, because the test-makers continue to tinker with the format. But the test in this book is as close as anyone can come without invoking lawyerly attention, and it will prepare you well for the real thing. As a bonus, you may find that preparing for the SAT improves your schoolwork, too, as you sharpen your reading skills, polish your grammar, and solve math problems more efficiently.

This book also uses a few special conventions. Keep them in mind as you work your way through this book:

- ✏ *Italics* have three different duties:

    - To introduce new terms, particularly those that apply to math, analytical reading, and writing

    - To refer to portions of a question or answer choice

    - To emphasize a particular word or point

- ✏ *This font* highlights words that may be useful when you take the SAT. Check out the definitions that follow these words, and notice the context. (Mastering words in context can really improve your score on the SAT.)

- ✏ **Boldface** indicates the action part of numbered steps and the main items in bulleted lists.

Foolish Assumptions

In writing this book, we assume several things about you, the reader, including the following:

- ✏ You probably hate standardized tests (nearly everybody does!) but want to achieve a high score on the SAT with minimum effort and maximum efficiency.

- ✏ You've taken the usual math and language arts courses through, say, algebra, geometry, and sophomore English. If you haven't taken one of those classes or if you did and still feel puzzled by the subject, you may want to read some other *For Dummies* books that can help you review the material. Take a look at *English Grammar For Dummies,* 2nd Edition, for basic information, or go for grammar practice with the *English Grammar Workbook For Dummies,* 2nd Edition and *1,001 Grammar Practice Questions For Dummies* (all written by Geraldine Woods). Those of you who struggle with the math will find these books helpful: *Algebra I For Dummies,* 2nd Edition, and *Algebra II For Dummies,* by Mary Jane Sterling, and *Geometry For Dummies,* 2nd Edition, by Mark Ryan. Wiley publishes all these titles.

One assumption we haven't made is age. True, most people who take the SAT are teenagers, but not everyone follows the same life path. If you're hitting college after living a little, good for you. This book can help you remember the schoolwork you need for the SAT, no matter how many years ago have passed since you sat in a classroom.

Icons Used in This Book

Icons are those cute little pictures that appear in the margins of this book. They indicate why you should pay special attention to the accompanying text. Here's how to decode them.

This icon points out helpful hints about strategy — what the all-star test-takers know and the rookies want to find out.

This icon identifies the sand traps that the SAT-writers are hoping you fall into as you take the test. Take note of these warnings so you know what to do (and what not to do) as you move from question to question on the real SAT.

When you see this icon, be sure to file away the information that accompanies it. The material will come in handy as you prepare for (and take) the 2016 SAT.

This icon identifies questions that resemble those on the actual SAT. Be sure to read the answer explanations that always follow the questions.

Where to Go from Here

Okay, now that you know what's what and where to find it, you have a choice. You can read every single word of Part I first and then take the practice exam, or you can check out only the parts of the book that address your "issues," as they say on daytime talk shows, concentrating on the kinds of questions you struggle with. (Check out Chapter 3 for an overview and sample questions similar to those on the exam.) If you're worried about when, where, and how to sign up and actually take the test, look through Chapters 1 and 2. Another good way to start is to take the sample test in Part II, score it using the appendix, and then focus on your weak spots. Feel free to check out www.dummies.com, where you'll find the "cheat sheet" (which is *not* for use during the exam) for *SAT For Dummies* and up-to-the-minute information on any changes the College Board has made to the test.

No matter what you do next, start by doing something simple: Calm down, stay loose, and score big on the SAT.

Part I
Getting Started
with the SAT

In this part . . .

- Get to know the new SAT. Find out what it tests, when you can and should take it, where you can find it, and how it affects your chances for admission to college.

- Find out how to best prepare yourself for success — from making the most of your time leading up to your testing date to ensuring you have what you need (and leaving home what you don't) on test day.

- Check out the redesigned SAT Reading, Writing and Language, and Math sections of the test and discover strategies to maximize your score on each one.

Chapter 1

Erasing the Worry: Getting to Know the New SAT

*I*n ancient Greek mythology — and in the Harry Potter series — a three-headed monster guards a magical place. In the real world, a different sort of three-headed monster — the SAT — protects another magical place: the college of your dreams. The SAT's three heads are tests of your skills in reading, writing, and math. Instead of chomping its victims like an imaginary monster, the SAT chops you up into a series of numbers — scores that play a *crucial* (extremely important) role in determining whether you receive a *please come to our school* or a *sorry to disappoint you* response at decision time.

In this chapter, you find the ABCs of the SAT: how it's changing as well as when, where, and how often you should take the test. This chapter also tells you what sort of scores you receive, explains how to deal with special needs, and gives you a peek into the structure of the exam itself.

Not an ACT: Getting Real with the SAT

Most college applicants take one of two giant exams on their way into U.S. colleges and some foreign schools. One is the ACT, and the other is the SAT. Most colleges accept scores from either test; check with the admissions office of the colleges on your list to be sure you're taking the test(s) they prescribe. (A good general rule for college admissions is to give them what they want, when they want it.) The SAT and the ACT are roughly the same in terms of difficulty, but each exam is of a different nature. As of this writing, you can access free PDFs from www.collegeboard.org and www.actstudent.org (homes of the SAT and ACT, respectively). If you're so inclined, you can download and review each exam and see which one you like more (or rather, which one you *dislike* less). Because you're reading *SAT For Dummies,* Quick Prep Edition, presumably you're taking the SAT. But if you're also taking the ACT, don't forget to check out *ACT For Dummies,* 6th Edition, by Lisa Zimmer Hatch, MA, and Scott A. Hatch, JD (Wiley).

Don't confuse the SAT with the SAT Subject Tests, which used to be called the SAT II, a name that is now officially *obsolete* (outdated, so yesterday). The SAT Subject Tests cover biology, history, math, and a ton of other stuff. Depending on the schools you apply to, you may have to take one or more Subject Tests or none at all.

All colleges have websites, where you can find out exactly which exam(s) your favorite schools require. Many libraries and nearly all bookstores also carry college guides — 20-pound paperbacks describing each and every institution of higher learning you may apply to. If you're relying on printed material, be sure to check the copyright date. With the *advent* (arrival) of the new SAT, some colleges may change their requirements, and earlier books may not be accurate. The official website of the College Board (www.collegeboard.org) also lists popular colleges and the tests they want to *inflict* (impose) on you. The College Board creates the exams, so its website is *replete* (well supplied) with helpful information.

If college isn't in your immediate future, you may want to take the SAT just to see how you do. If your plans include a stint in the armed forces or climbing Mount Everest before hitting higher education, you can keep your options open by taking the SAT before you go. Your score on the SAT may be higher while formal "book learning" is still fresh in your mind. Then when you're ready to return to an actual classroom education, you have some scores to send to the college of your choice, though if a long period of time has passed, the college may ask for a retest. How long is *a long period of time?* It depends on the college you're applying to. Some may ask for an updated score after only a couple of years; others are more *lenient* (easygoing). Obviously, whether you took three years off to relax on the beach or five to create a gazillion-dollar Internet company also influences the admissions office's decision on SAT scores. Check with the college(s) you're interested in and explain your situation.

A Whole New Ballgame: Comparing the Old and New SAT

What a difference a couple of months make! If you take the SAT in January 2016 and then again in March 2016, the exams you face will *not* be identical twins. Like any family members, they may share the arch of an eyebrow or the shape of the nose, but otherwise they're quite different. Check out Table 1-1 for a side-by-side comparison of the old and new exams.

Table 1-1	Old SAT versus New SAT
Old SAT	*New SAT*
Critical Reading: 67 questions, 70 minutes	Reading: 52 questions, 65 minutes
Essay: Mandatory, 25 minutes, respond to a prompt with your own point of view and evidence	Essay: Optional, 50 minutes, analyze writing techniques in a passage
Multiple-Choice Writing: 49 questions, 60 minutes	Multiple-Choice Writing and Language: 44 questions, 35 minutes
Mathematics: 54 questions, 70 minutes, divided into 3 sections	Mathematics: 57 questions, 80 minutes, divided into 2 sections
Calculators allowed for all 3 sections	Calculators allowed for 1 section and not for the other

Old SAT	New SAT
Multiple-Choice and Grid-In Scoring: 1 point for each correct answer, 1/4-point deduction for each wrong multiple-choice answer (no penalty for incorrect grid-in answers)	Multiple-Choice and Grid-In Scoring: 1 point for each correct answer, no deduction for wrong answers
Multiple-Choice Format: 5 possible answers	Multiple-Choice Format: 4 possible answers
Score Types: 200–800 points each for Critical Reading, Writing, and Mathematics (total: 600–2400 points)	Score Types: 200–800 points for a combination of the Reading and Writing and Language sections; another 200–800 points for Mathematics, for a total of 400–1600 for the entire exam, separate essay score, cross-test subscores for analysis in history and science, section subscores for various skills

Now you know the basics. For more information on the changes to the SAT, see the section "Examining Your Mind: What the New SAT Tests," later in this chapter.

Signing Up Before Sitting Down: Registering for the SAT

The SAT is given at multiple times at select high schools throughout the United States and in English-speaking schools in many other countries. Home-schoolers can also take the SAT, though not in their own living rooms. This section explains how and when to register for an exam and acceptable methods of payment. *Note:* The SAT *waives* (drops) fees for low-income test-takers. Check out the section "Meeting Special Needs" in this chapter for more information.

How to register

You can register for the SAT online, by mail, or, if you've taken the SAT before, by phone.

Online registration is simple: Go to www.sat.collegeboard.org/register to sign up and to choose a test center and date. You need a credit card or a PayPal account and a digital photo of yourself ready to upload. Be sure the photo meets the College Board's *criteria* (standards). The College Board wants what Hollywood agents call "a head shot" — a photo featuring everything above shoulder level. You should be the only one in the picture, and your whole face must be visible. Head coverings are okay only if they're religious in nature. The College Board accepts JPEG, GIF, and PNG formats.

You can also register by mail. In fact, you have to do so if you're younger than 13 or older than 21 or if you need to take the exam on a Sunday for religious reasons. Ask the college or guidance counselor at your school for a registration form. If you're home-schooled, call the nearest public or private high school. Older test-takers (over 21 years of age): Call the College Board Customer Service Center for help (within the U.S.: 866-756-7346; outside the U.S.: 212-713-7789). You have to attach a photo (no smaller than 2 x 2 inches and no larger than 2.5 x 3 inches) to the paper registration. Follow the same guidelines for the online photo, and make sure it shows your face clearly. Tape the photo to the designated area of the application. With the application, enclose payment (credit card number, a check from a United States bank, or a bank draft).

If you're suffering through the SAT for a second time, you can register by phone, though you pay an extra $15 to do so. Call the College Board's Customer Service center (within the U.S.: 866-756-7346; outside the U.S.: 212-713-7789). Hearing-impaired test-takers can call the TTY Customer Service number (within the U.S.: 888-857-2477; outside the U.S.: 609-882-4118).

However you register, you'll be asked whether you want to sign up for the Student Search Service. Answer yes and fill out the questionnaire. Colleges, universities, and some scholarship-granting organizations receive information about you from this service. Expect lots of emails and letters — a little annoying, perhaps, but you may discover a school or scholarship that meets your needs perfectly.

Neither the Student Search Service nor any other part of the College Board markets products to you via email or regular mail, but some scam artists do. Don't send personal or financial information to any organization unless you know it's legitimate. Not sure? Call the College Board to check (within the U.S.: 866-756-7346; outside the U.S.: 212-713-7789).

When you register for the SAT, you also choose the type of score reports you want to receive. See the section "Scoring on the New SAT," later in this chapter, to explore your options.

When to take the test

The last "old" SAT is scheduled for January 2016; the first "new" SAT debuts in March 2016. Keep those dates in mind as you make your own personal test schedule.

The SAT pops up on the calendar seven times a year. You can take the exam as often as you want. If you're a *masochist* — that is, you enjoy pain — you can take all seven tests, but most people stick to this schedule:

- **Autumn of junior year** (about 1¾ years before college entrance): Time to take the PSAT/NMSQT, the exam that serves as a preview of the real thing. Even if you don't believe you need a preview, take the PSAT/NMSQT anyway; this test serves as a sorting tool for several scholarship opportunities and special programs. The first redesigned PSAT/NMSQT will be given in October 2015.

- **Spring of junior year** (about 1¼ years before college entrance): Take the SAT strictly for practice, though you can send in your scores if you're pleased with them.

- **Autumn of senior year** (a bit less than a year before entrance): The SAT strikes again. Early-decision candidates should take the test in October or November; regular applicants may choose from any of the three autumn dates, including December.

- **Winter of senior year** (half-year before entrance): Some SAT-lovers take the exam in autumn and again in winter, hoping that practice will make them perfect, at least in the eyes of the colleges. The high scores won't hurt (and you probably will improve, just because the whole routine will be familiar), but don't put a lot of energy into repeated bouts of SAT fever. Your grades and extracurriculars may suffer if you're too *fixated on* (obsessed with) the SAT, and you may end up hurting your overall application.

If you're transferring or starting your college career midyear, you may sit for the SAT in January, March, May, or June. Check with your counselor or with the college of your choice and go with that recommendation.

Everyone takes the SAT on Saturday except for those students who can't for religious reasons. If you fall into that category, your SAT will be on a Sunday following a Saturday SAT day. Get a letter from your *cleric* (religious leader) on letterhead and mail it in with your registration form.

In terms of test sites, the early bird gets the worm. (Do you ever wonder why no one talks about the worm? He got up early, too, and look what happened to him.) When you register, you may request a test site, but if it's filled, you get an alternate. So don't delay; send in the form or register online as soon as you know when and where you want to take the exam.

Meeting Special Needs

In a speech introducing the redesigned SAT, the president of the College Board stressed fairness and equal access for all students, including those with special needs. Even if you don't think you belong in that category, skim this section. You may discover an option that will help you "show what you know" when it matters most.

Learning disabilities

If you have a learning disability, you may be allowed to take the SAT under special conditions. The first step is to get an Eligibility Form from your school counselor. (Home-schoolers, call the local high school.) You may also want to ask your college counseling or guidance office for a copy of the *College Board Services for Students with Disabilities Brochure* (pamphlet). If your school doesn't have one, contact the College Board directly (212-713-8333, TTY 609-882-4118) or check the testing agency's website (www.collegeboard.org/students-with-disabilities). You can also contact the College Board by mail at this address: College Board SSD Program, P.O. Box 8060, Mount Vernon, IL 62864-0060.

After you've been certified for accommodations on one College Board test (an AP, a SAT Subject Test, or the PSAT/NMSQT), you're certified for all, unless your need arises from a temporary medical condition. If you fall into that category, see the next section for more information.

File the form well in advance of the time you expect to take the test. Generally, if you're entitled to extra test time in your high school, you'll be eligible for extra time on the SAT. What does *extra time* really mean? Extra time equals 1½ the usual amount for each section. So if regular test-takers have 50 minutes to write the essay, for example, extended-timers get 75 minutes.

¡Atención! What every foreign student needs to know about the new SAT

First, welcome to the U.S.'s worst invention, the Seriously Annoying Test (SAT), which you're taking so that you can attend an American institution. Getting ready for this exam may make you consider another American institution, one with padded rooms and bars on the windows. But a high score on the new exam is certainly within reach for individuals who have studied English as a second language. Because the new SAT tests vocabulary in context, you can usually figure out the answer, even if you don't know the formal definition, by plugging in a *plausible* (reasonable) alternative word. As a foreign student, pay special attention to the vocabulary words in this book, which, like *plausible*, are defined in context. You may want to keep a notebook or a computer file of new words you come across as you work through the sample questions. Also, a number of questions on the new SAT involve visual data in the form of graphs, charts, and diagrams. These require little knowledge of English.

Be sure to turn your concentration up to "totally intense" in the math section of this chapter and Chapter 3 because arithmetic doesn't change from language to language. Neither does geometry or algebra. If you can crack the basic language used to put forth the problem, you should be able to score a ton of points.

Physical issues

At no additional charge, the SAT also provides wheelchair accessibility, large-print tests, and other accommodations for students who need them. The key is to submit the Eligibility Form early so that the College Board can ask for suitable documentation and set up appropriate test conditions for you. You can send paper documentation or file an Eligibility Form via the Internet. Check out www.collegeboard.com/students-with-disabilities for details.

If a physical problem (a broken arm, perhaps) occurs shortly before your scheduled SAT and you can't easily take the exam at a later date, call the College Board (212-713-8333, TTY 609-882-4118), explain the situation, and have your physician fill out the forms requesting whatever accommodation you need.

Questions about special needs? Your high school's counselor or principal can help, or you can email the College Board (ssd@info.collegeboard.org).

Financial help

If your special need resides in your wallet, you can apply for a fee waiver, which is available to low-income high-school juniors and seniors who live in the United States, Puerto Rico, and other American territories. (United States citizens living in other countries may also be eligible for fee waivers.) Not only does the College Board waive its fee for the exam, but it also gives you four extra score reports for free. And, as they say on television infomercials, "Wait! There's more!" When you apply to college, you usually have to pay an application fee. If the College Board has waived its fee, you receive four request forms for college application fee-waivers. Not a bad deal!

For any financial issues, check with your school counselor for fee-waiver applications. (As with everything to do with the SAT, if you're a home-schooler, call the local high school for a form.) And be careful to avoid additional fees when you can. You run into extra charges for late or changed registration and for some extras — super-speedy scores, an analysis of your performance, and the like. (See the section "Scoring on the SAT," later in this chapter, for more information on score-reporting options.)

Examining Your Mind: What the New SAT Tests

Reality isn't just material for television shows anymore. It takes a starring role in the redesigned SAT. Nearly all the changes on the exam attempt to measure the skills you need to succeed in school and in the workplace. Gone are questions that fall into the "guessing game" category — sentence completions and recognition of grammar mistakes in random sentences, for instance. Questions on the new SAT tend to be longer and to rely more closely on the most common elements of the average school's curriculum.

That said, the SAT is still just a snapshot of your mental *prowess* (ability) on one weekend morning. College admissions offices are well aware of this fact. No matter how *rigorous* (tough, demanding) your high school is, other factors may influence your score, such as whether you deal easily with multiple-choice questions and how you feel physically and mentally on SAT day (fight with Mom? bad romance? week-old sushi?). Bottom line: Stop obsessing about the SAT's unfairness (and it is unfair) and prepare.

The college admission essay is a great place to put your scores in perspective. If you face some special circumstances, such as a learning disability, a school that doesn't value academics, a family tragedy, and so on, you may want to explain your situation in an essay. No essay wipes out the bad impression created by an extremely low SAT score, but a good essay gives the college a way to interpret your achievement and to see you, the applicant, in more detail. For help with the college admission essay, check out *College Admission Essays For Dummies,* by Geraldine Woods (published by Wiley).

The SAT doesn't test facts you studied in school; you don't need to know when Columbus sailed across the Atlantic or how to calculate the molecular weight of magnesium to answer an SAT question. Instead, the SAT takes aim at your ability to follow a logical sequence, to comprehend what you've read, and to write clearly in Standard English. The math portion checks whether you were paying attention or snoring when little details like algebra were taught. Check out the following sections for a bird's-eye view of the three SAT topics.

Reading

This portion of the exam used to be called Critical Reading, but for some reason the test-writers dropped half of the name. However, reading-comprehension passages still play a *critical* (vital, essential) role in your SAT score. Besides dropping sentence completions — statements with blanks and five possible ways to fill them — reading-comprehension questions now ask you to choose among four, not five, possible answers. Here's what you see on the new SAT Reading section:

- ✔ **Quantity:** A total of four single passages plus one set of paired passages, each from 500 to 750 words long, with each passage or pair accompanied by 10 to 11 questions, for a total of 52 questions.

- ✔ **Content:** Two passages, or one passage and one pair, in science; one literary passage, either narrative fiction or nonfiction; and two passages, or one passage and one pair, in history/social studies. One of the history/social studies passages or pair deals with what the College Board calls the "Great Global Conversation" — a historical document, such as a presidential speech or a modern discussion of an issue relating to democracy and human rights.

- ✔ **Reading level:** Some passages on the 9th and 10th grade level, some on the college-entry level (12th grade and beyond).

- ✔ **Graphics:** Charts, tables, graphs, diagrams: one to two in science, and one to two in history/social studies.

Reading-comprehension questions are a mixture of literal (just the facts, ma'am) and interpretive/analytical. You'll be asked to choose the meaning of a word in context and to understand information presented graphically (though you don't need to know math to answer these questions). You may also have to assess the author's tone or point of view. At least two questions per passage or pair ask you to recognize supporting evidence for your answer. Take a look at this pair of questions.

Tim was frantic to learn that the first GC-MP8 handheld was already in circulation. And here he was wasting his time in college! The degree that he had pursued so doggedly for the past three years now seemed nothing more than a gigantic waste of time. The business world, that's where he belonged, marketing someone else's technology with just enough of a twist to allow him to patent "his" idea. Yes, Tim now knew what he must do: Spend time with YouTube until he found an inventor unlikely to sue Tim for intellectual property theft.

In this passage, the word *his* is in quotation marks

(A) because it's a pronoun

(B) because the reader is supposed to hiss at Tim, whom everyone hates

(C) to show that the idea is really someone else's

(D) because the typesetter had some extra quotation marks

The best evidence for the answer to the preceding question is

(A) "Tim was frantic . . . circulation."

(B) "The degree . . . years now"

(C) "The business world . . . belonged"

(D) "marketing someone else's . . . twist"

Note: In the real exam, the lines will be numbered and the questions will include the line they're interested in.

The answer to the first question is Choice (C). These quotation marks refer to Tim's claim to "someone else's technology." Although he isn't quoted directly, the quotation marks around *his* imply that Tim says that a particular invention is his, when in fact it isn't.

The answer to the second question is Choice (D). As you see in the explanation to the first question, these words reveal that the technology isn't Tim's invention and support the correct answer, *to show that the idea is really someone else's.*

Writing and language

To the *chagrin* (disappointment or embarrassment) of English teachers everywhere, the new SAT Writing and Language section contains even less actual writing: one optional 50-minute essay analyzing the writing style of a passage you've never seen before plus 35 minutes' worth of short answers. Why so little writing? As those of us who sit with four-foot-high piles of essays on our laps know, it takes a long time to read student prose. The SAT test-makers must pay people to read and score essays — a much more expensive and time-consuming proposition than running a bubble sheet through a scanner. Here are the details.

The essay

The prompt, or question, never changes, but the passage does. You have to figure out the author's point of view, what he or she is arguing for or against. Then you must pick apart the passage, discussing *how* the author attempts to persuade the reader to accept this point of view. Finally, you get 50 minutes to write your own essay, describing what you've discovered. Your own ideas on the subject, by the way, are *irrelevant* (beside the point). The College Board doesn't care what you think; graders simply want to know whether you can identify the relationship between style and content in someone else's work.

Many standardized tests may now be taken on a computer. The College Board has begun to move toward a computer-based SAT, too, at the speed of an elderly turtle. As of this writing, the computer-based SAT will be available at only a few sites. The College Board promises that at some point it will be everywhere. When? Don't hold your breath! No date has been given, and the College Board has never been famous for its speed in technical innovation. Currently, only those who have been certified as *dysgraphic* (having a learning disability that affects handwriting) may type the essay. For everyone else, handwriting is your only option. Start practicing your penmanship.

Multiple-choice questions

You get four passages, each from 400 to 450 words long, accompanied by 11 questions per passage. The passages represent fairly good student writing, but they all have room for improvement in grammar, punctuation, organization, logic, and style. The multiple-choice questions address those areas. In terms of content, you see one passage in each of these areas: careers, history/social studies, humanities, and science. One or two passages will make an argument for a particular idea, one or two may be informative or explanatory, and one will be a narrative. At least one passage (and probably more) includes a graphic element — a chart, table, diagram or graph relating to the subject matter. One question checks that the passage accurately represents the information in the graphic element. The questions may focus on a single word (to check your vocabulary-in-context skill) or on the passage as a whole (to determine your ability to organize information).

Take a look at this example, which, on the real exam, would be part of a longer passage. Which answer best changes the underlined portion of the sentence?

Having been turned down by 15 major league baseball teams, Milton changed to basketball, and he succeeded <u>in his goal where he was aiming to be a professional athlete.</u>

(A) NO CHANGE

(B) in that he reached his goal of aiming to be a professional athlete

(C) where he became a professional athlete

(D) in his goal of becoming a professional athlete

The answer is Choice (D), because that version conveys the information smoothly and correctly. Did you notice that Choice (A) keeps the wording of the original passage? That's the design in most multiple-choice Writing and Language questions.

Mathematics

SAT math questions rely on Algebra II and some advanced topics in geometry, statistics, probability, and trigonometry. The new SAT Mathematics section contains one 55-minute section when you can use a calculator and one 25-minute section when you can't. Of the 57 questions, 45 are multiple-choice, in which you choose an answer from four possibilities, and 12 are *grid-ins*, in which you supply an answer and bubble in the actual number, not a multiple-choice letter. Whether calculator or no calculator, multiple-choice or grid-in answer, each question is worth the same except for one grid-in question called Extended Thinking, which carries four times the weight of the other math questions. Here's a sample multiple-choice problem:

If $xy - 12 = z$, and the value of x is 2, which of the following must be true?

(A) $z = xy$

(B) $y = 12 + z$

(C) $z = 2y - 12$

(D) $2y - z = 100$

Substitute 2 for x, and see which answer most closely resembles $2y - 12 = z$. The correct answer is Choice (C).

Scoring on the New SAT

The new SAT has a completely different scoring system. The goal is to give colleges an in-depth look at your performance. Scared? Don't be. If you take the exam more than once, as most people do, you can use the detailed information from your score reports to craft a personalized study program, zeroing in on the skills you need to *hone* (sharpen).

Types of scores

The redesigned SAT gives you many, many more scores than the older exam. Here's the deal:

- **Composite score:** This is the sum of Reading, Writing and Language, and Mathematics (400 to 1600 points). The maximum SAT score is 1600 (with a top score of 800 on Reading and Writing and Language and 800 on Mathematics). The minimum is 400, which you get for little more than showing up and bubbling in a few ovals *randomly* (without a plan or reason).

- **Area scores:** These are the scores for Reading and Writing and Language (200 to 800 points) and Mathematics (200 to 800 points). The optional essay receives a separate score, still being fine-tuned but probably 3 to 12 points.

- **Test scores:** This name, *bestowed* (given) by the College Board, is a little surprising, because where else would your scores come from, other than the test? This is the term applied to the three branches of the exam. You get a score for Reading (10 to 40 points), Writing and Language (10 to 40 points), and Mathematics (10 to 40 points).

- **Cross-test:** These scores are determined by questions of a particular type in all three areas of the SAT (Reading, Writing and Language, and Mathematics). You get a score for analysis in history/social studies (10 to 40 points) and another for analysis in science (10 to 40 points).

- **Subscores:** A few skills on the new SAT are so important and *ubiquitous* (appearing everywhere) that the College Board provides separate scores for them. On the Reading and Writing and Language sections, you get a score for command of evidence (1 to 15 points) and understanding words in context (1 to 15 points). On the Writing and Language section, you get a score for expression of ideas (1 to 15 points) and Standard English conventions (1 to 15 points). The scoring of the essay will evolve as results from the first few new SATs come in. The current plan is to provide three subscores (reading, analysis, writing), each 2 to 8 points, based on adding the scores of two readers who grade your essay from 1 to 4 in those categories. The Mathematics section gives you three scores: 1 to 15 points each for algebra, advanced math, and problem solving/data analysis.

One happy, wonderful development is that the new SAT has no penalty for wrong answers! You get one point for each correct answer you supply, and no deduction for incorrect answers. This system does away with a "trick" of the old SAT — gaming the system by guessing when the odds favored you and skipping a question when they didn't. Now you can answer every question, even if you're clueless, unless you run out of time.

Score reporting

The basic fee for the test includes four score reports. Students who are eligible for a fee waiver can request an additional four free reports. You send these reports to colleges you're interested in. If you want to add still more colleges to your list, you can do so by paying $11.25 extra for each additional score report. (Prices, of course, are always subject to change, and don't expect any to go down. Check the College Board website at www.collegeboard.org for pricing changes.) You request additional score reports on the Additional Score Report Request Form (how do they think of these names?), which you can download from the website.

For a higher fee ($13.50), you can get a detailed analysis of your test performance — how many of each sort of question you answered right and wrong and how difficult each question was. Then you can tailor your prep hours to the stuff that's hard for you. Ask for the Student Answer Service when you register. For even more money ($18), the SAT sends you a copy of the questions and the correct answers. Fee waivers apply to this service.

If you're planning to take another SAT, spring for the Student Answer Service. Seeing what you got wrong gives you a blueprint for review.

Score reports arrive in your mailbox and at your high school about five weeks after you take the test. If you're the antsy type and are willing to fork over a few more dollars, you can find out the good news by phone. Call Customer Service (within the U.S.: 866-756-7346; outside the U.S.: 212-713-7789; TTY 888-857-2477 for the U.S. or 609-882-4118 for outside the U.S.). Have a credit card, your registration number, and your birth date ready. The fee for a "rush" score is $15. If you're returning to academia after a break and want access to old scores, you pay $31 for the College Board to dig them up.

If you have access to the Internet, you can create a free (yes, something's actually free!) account on the College Board website (www.collegeboard.com). Look for My SAT Online Score Report. It tells you your 200 to 800 scores in Reading, Writing and Language, and Mathematics and some information on how well you did on various types of questions. The report also tells you how well your performance was in comparison with everyone else who took the exam when you did.

Chapter 2

Slow and Steady (Breathing) Wins the Race: Preparing for the Test

In This Chapter

▶ Tailoring SAT prep to your life

▶ Using the time remaining before the test efficiently

▶ Dealing with last-minute nerves

▶ Ensuring success on the morning of the test

"*A*ll things are ready, if our mind be so," wrote William Shakespeare. When you hit test day, the last thing you want is an unprepared mind. But you won't have one, because this chapter explains how to make "all things . . . ready," especially your mind, for the SAT.

SAT prep can start at many different points in your life and still be effective. In this chapter, you find long-term and short-term strategies for SAT prep as well as medium-length prep for the Average Joe and Josephine. And for those of you who suddenly realized that the test is *next week*, here you find a panic-button scenario. Lastly, this chapter tells you what to do to maximize your score the night before the test (speaking of panic) as well as the morning of SAT day.

Starting Early: A Long-Range Plan

You're the type of person who buys summer clothes in December. (By the way, thanks a lot. Because of you, all the department stores feature bikinis when normal people are trying to buy sweaters.) To put it another way, you're not in diapers, but the test isn't coming up within the next year. Congratulations. Check out the following long-range SAT-prep plan:

✔ **Sign up for challenging courses in school.** If you're in high school, *eschew* (reject) courses that require papers short enough to tweet and just enough math to figure out how many minutes remain before your next vacation. Go for subjects that stretch your mind. Specifically, stick it out with math at least through Algebra II. If high school is in your rearview mirror, check out extension or enrichment adult-ed courses.

✔ **Get into the habit of reading.** Cereal boxes, Internet pop-up balloons, and 1,000-page novels — they're all good, though they're not all equal. The more you read, and the more difficult the material you read, the more your reading comprehension improves. The new SAT places special emphasis on two reading skills — understanding vocabulary in context and analyzing evidence. In all your assigned or leisure reading, take note of unfamiliar words. Try to figure out the definition from the surrounding material, and then check yourself by looking up the word in a standard dictionary or online dictionary or by questioning a handy teacher or parent. (Your peers may know also, but they'll think you're strange if you ask vocab questions!) Also notice *how* the author makes a point — through description, quotations from experts, word choice, and so forth. Then when you encounter a question about evidence on the SAT, you'll know how to respond. Studying writing style also preps you for the optional SAT essay.

✔ **Write to the editor.** The editor of anything! Find a point of view and start sending off your prose — to the school or local paper, to websites, or to television stations. By practicing argumentative skills (and, yes, you can use them to fight with authority figures in your personal life!), you learn to recognize writing techniques in SAT reading and writing passages. As a side benefit, you may have a civic impact.

✔ **Be aware of graphics.** You don't have to be Picasso, but you do have to understand how tables, charts, graphs, diagrams, and other visuals *convey* (communicate) information. The new SAT awards many points to those who can correctly interpret graphic elements. Pay attention to illustrations when you're studying science, history, and math or reading something that has nothing to do with school.

✔ **Keep your math notebooks.** Resist the urge to burn your geometry text the minute the last class is over. Keep your math notebooks and (if you're really motivated!) folders of homework papers. Don't throw out any old exams. From time to time, go over the important concepts, because these are what you'll need on the SAT. Research shows that memory improves when concepts are reviewed after a period of time. The SAT math doesn't go in depth into any one topic, but the questions do require you to be *proficient* (skilled) with the basics. Review your notebooks to stay current with multiplying exponents, the Pythagorean theorem, and $y = mx + b$.

✔ **Read Chapter 3 carefully so you understand the structure of each type of SAT question.** When SAT day dawns, you shouldn't be facing any surprises. Be sure that you're familiar with the directions for each section so that you don't have to waste time reading them during the actual exam.

✔ **Take the practice exam in Part II of this book.** Work your way through all those questions and then check the answers and explanations to everything you got wrong, skipped, or wobbled on. After you identify your weak spots (not that you actually have any — just areas where you could be even more excellent), you know what you have to practice.

✔ **Take the PSAT/NMSQT.** This "mini-SAT" gives you a chance to experience test conditions. It may also open the door to several pretty snazzy scholarships, such as the National Merit (the "NM" in the title of the test). The new PSAT/NMSQT, which is changing along with the SAT, debuts in October 2015. You'll get a preview of what you face on the redesigned SAT.

As the SAT approaches, you long-range planners can relax. You're in a fine position to *condescend* (act superior) to all the goof-offs who didn't even begin to think about the exam until junior year in high school. What? You're one of those goof-offs? Never fear. Hope and help arrive in the next section.

Avoiding Extremes: A Medium-Range Plan

In this category, you're conscientious but not obsessive. You have less than a year before SAT day, and you have a reasonable amount of time to devote to SAT prep. Here's your strategy:

✔ **Do all you can to sharpen your reading skills during your last school year before the SAT.** Remember that reading-comprehension skills matter in all three sections of the exam (Reading, Writing and Language, and Mathematics). When you're doing your homework or surfing the web, make friends with words (not to be confused with the app Words with Friends). Jot down unfamiliar words and examine the context. Can you determine the meaning? If not, hit the dictionary or *query* (question) someone who knows. If you have a spare hour, try a crossword puzzle — a great way to learn new words! *Peruse* (read thoroughly, scrutinize) the newspaper every day, either online or on paper, and check out the way in which statistics appear. Be sure to read the opinion columns and analyze how the author argues a point.

✔ **Work on your writing.** If your school offers an elective in nonfiction writing, go for it. Consider writing for the school newspaper. Send letters or emails to the editor (see a fuller explanation in the section "Starting Early: A Long-Range Plan"). Become comfortable with the sort of writing that makes a case for a particular point of view, because that's what you have to analyze on the new SAT — in the essay, multiple-choice writing, and reading sections.

✔ **Get a math study-buddy.** I'm not talking about a tutor. Yes, you can learn a lot from someone who dreams quadratic equations, but you can also benefit from studying with someone who is on your own level of ability. As the two of you work together, solving problems and reviewing formulas, you can practice and set the knowledge firmly into your brain. All teachers know that you learn best what you have to explain to someone else. Plus, a study-buddy probably can explain what he or she knows in a different way. If the teacher's explanation didn't do it for you, your friend's may.

✔ *Resurrect* **(bring forth again) your Algebra II book or borrow one from a friendly math teacher.** Look through the chapters that you struggled with the first time you went through the book. Refresh your memory with a sample problem or two.

✔ **Study the illustrations in your science and history textbooks.** Many questions on all three parts of the new SAT include graphic elements. You may see a chart of voting preferences, a graph representing bacterial growth, or a map of cultivated land. Learning to decode these illustrations — as well as similar illustrations in material you read outside of school (you *do* read other material, right?) — helps you ace the SAT.

✔ **Look through Chapter 3.** Read the explanations of each type of question. Be sure that you know the directions and format by heart.

✔ **Take the practice exam in Part II of this book.** Pay special attention to the explanations accompanying each question that puzzled you (even if you accidentally got the right answer!). After you know which sort of question is likely to stump you, practice the skills underlying those questions. For example, you may discover that your grammar is a bit rusty. Time to hit your grammar book, or, if you don't have one, practice with *English Grammar Workbook For Dummies* or *1,001 Grammar Practice Questions For Dummies* (both published by Wiley).

✔ **Take the PSAT/NMSQT.** You can't pass up a chance to experience the exam in its native habitat (a testing center), even if the test is shorter than the real SAT. Beginning in October 2015, the PSAT/NMSQT resembles the design of the new SAT.

If you follow this plan, you should be in fine shape for the SAT, and, as a bonus, you'll have time for an actual life, too.

Cutting It Close: A Short-Range Plan

The SAT is next month or (gulp!) next week. Not ideal, but not hopeless either. Use the following plan to get through it alive:

✔ **Read Chapter 3 of this book carefully.** Find out what sort of questions are on the exam.

✔ **Do the practice exam from Part II.** Yes, it's terrible. Nearly four good hours gone forever. But you should do the exam anyway, just so you know what the SAT experience is like.

Should you take an SAT prep course?

Complete this sentence: SAT prep courses

(A) don't make a huge difference in your score

(B) employ Ivy League graduates who are paying off college loans until their blogs go viral

(C) provide jobs for unemployed doctoral candidates finishing dissertations on the sex life of bacteria

(D) keep underpaid high-school teachers from total *penury* (poverty)

The answer: All of the above. Choices (B) through (D) don't need an explanation, but you're probably wondering about Choice (A). The College Board, which makes the exam, has studied the effects of SAT prep courses and found that in general they have a minimal effect on your score. A few long-term courses do make a slightly bigger difference (25 to 40 points combined on the old SAT's verbal and math sections), but because you have to devote 40-plus hours to them, you get approximately one extra point per hour of study. Not a very efficient use of your time! You've already proved your brilliance by purchasing *SAT For Dummies*, Quick Prep Edition. If you work your way through the book with some care, you've done enough.

✔ **Read the explanations for *all* the questions on the practice test.** The explanations give you not only the correct answer but also some general information that will take your skills up a notch with minimal effort and time.

✔ **Clear the deck of all unnecessary activity so you can study as much as possible.** Don't skip your sister's wedding (or your physics homework), but if you can put something off, do so. Use the extra time to practice skills emphasized on the SAT. (Chapter 3 identifies those skills.)

Sometimes students put themselves in danger of failing a course in school because they're spending all their homework time on SAT prep. Bad idea. Yes, you want to send good scores to the colleges of your choice, but you also want to send a decent high-school transcript. Prepare for the test, but do your homework, too.

Coping with SAT-Night Fever

No matter what, don't study on SAT day minus one. The only thing that last-minute studying does is make you more nervous. What happens is simple: The closer you get to test day, the more you take notice of the stuff you don't know. On the eve of the test, every unfamiliar vocabulary word is outlined in neon, as is every *obscure* (not well known, hidden) math formula. And every time you find something that you don't know — or forget something that you did know at one time — your heart beats a little faster. Panic doesn't equal a good night's sleep, and eight solid hours of snoozing is the best possible prep for three-plus hours of multiple-choice questions.

Also, resist the urge to contact your friends who are also taking the test. Chances are they're nervous, and every text is a potential anxiety-propeller. Instead, place everything you need in the morning in one spot, ready and waiting for use. Lay out some comfortable clothes, preferably layers. If the test room is too cold, you want to be able to add a sweater. If it's too hot, you may find removing a jacket or sweater helpful without getting arrested for indecent exposure.

After you set up everything for SAT day, do something that's fun . . . but not too much fun. No parties or clubs for you! Find an activity that eases you through the last couple of pre-SAT waking hours. Go to sleep at a reasonable time (after setting your alarm clock) and dream of little, penciled ovals patting you gently on the shoulder.

Getting there is half the fun

On the morning of the SAT, what should you avoid more than anything?

(A) a relaxing session of your favorite cartoons

(B) a two-hour detour on the road to the test center

(C) a kiss from Grandma

(D) a slurp from your dog

The answer is Choice (B). Did you ever watch an old sitcom on television, one with a pregnancy plotline? Inevitably, the mad dash to the hospital is lengthened by a detour, a traffic jam, or a wrong turn. On SAT day, you don't want to be in that old sitcom. Make sure that your journey to the test center is event-free. Try the route there at least once before test day, preferably at the same time and on the same day of the week (that is, Saturday morning, unless you're taking the test on Sunday because of religious observances) so you know what sort of traffic to expect. Leave the house with plenty of time to spare. The idea is to arrive rested and as relaxed as someone who is facing 200-plus minutes of test can be.

Smoothing Out SAT-Day Morning

SAT day isn't a good time to oversleep. Set the alarm clock and ask a reliable parent/ guardian/friend to verify that you've awakened on time. If you're not a morning person, you may need a few additional minutes. Then, no matter how nutritionally challenged your usual breakfast is, eat something healthful. Unless it upsets your stomach, go for protein (eggs, cheese, meat, tofu, and so on). Stay away from sugary items (cereals made primarily from Red Dye No. 23, corn syrup, and the like) because sugar gives you a surge of energy and then a large chunk of fatigue. You don't want your sugar-high to *plummet* (fall sharply) right in the middle of a math section. Then hit the road for the test center.

If disaster strikes — fever, car trouble, uncle's arrest — and you can't take the SAT on the appointed day, call the College Board and request that they transfer your fee to the next available date.

Bringing the right stuff

On the day of the test, before you leave for the testing center, be sure you have these items with you:

- ✓ **Admission ticket for the SAT:** Don't leave home without it! If you registered online, print out the ticket. If you registered by mail or phone, check with the College Board a week or so before the test if your ticket still hasn't arrived. You can't get in just by swearing that you "have the ticket at home on top of the TV, really."

- ✓ **Photo identification:** The SAT accepts drivers' licenses, school IDs, passports, or other official documents that include your picture. The SAT doesn't accept Social Security cards or library cards. If you're not sure what to bring, ask your school counselor or check the College Board website (www.collegeboard.org).

- ✓ **No. 2 pencils:** Don't guess. Look for the No. 2 on the side of the pencil. Take at least three or four sharpened pencils with you. Be sure the pencils have usable erasers or bring one of those cute pink rubber erasers you used in elementary school.

- ✓ **Calculator:** Bringing a calculator is optional but recommended. You don't absolutely need a calculator to take the SAT, but it does help on some questions. A four-function, scientific, or graphing calculator is acceptable. The day before the exam, make sure the batteries in your calculator work. Anything with a keyboard (a mini-computer, in other words), a phone, or an iPad is barred, as are other tablets or any device that uses a stylus to input information. Also banned is anything that needs to be plugged in or that makes noise.

- ✔ **Handkerchief or tissues:** Experienced test-takers know that absolutely nothing is more annoying than a continuous drip or sniffle. Blow your nose and do the rest of the room — and yourself — a favor!

- ✔ **Snacks:** Bring some healthy snacks (some trail mix, cheese, or other non-candy items) in your backpack. You can eat them during your rest breaks.

- ✔ **Watch:** Yes, they still make watches, and no, you can't use your phone to check the time. Borrow a watch from somebody old enough to own one in case the wall clock is missing, broken, or out of your line of vision. Don't bring one that beeps because the proctor may take it away if it disturbs other test-takers.

After you arrive at the test center, take out what you need and stow the rest of the stuff in a backpack under your seat.

You're not allowed to bring a phone, camera, computer, or tablet to the testing room. Nor can you bring scrap paper, books, and other school supplies (rulers, compasses, highlighters, and so on). Leave these items behind. Also, no portable music devices. If your "watch" is one of those new, wearable computers, leave it home!

Easing test tension

You'll probably feel nervous when you arrive at the test center. Try a couple of stretches and head shakes to *dispel* (chase away) tension. During the exam, wriggle your feet and move your shoulders up and down whenever you feel yourself tightening up. Some people like neck rolls (pretend that your neck is made of spaghetti and let your head droop in a big circle). If you roll your neck or move your head to either side, however, be sure to close your eyes. Don't risk a charge of cheating. Just like an Olympic diver preparing to go off of the board, take a few deep breaths to calm yourself.

Recent studies have shown that some tension can actually boost your score. Before you begin the exam, visualize a time when you were nervous and had a good outcome — say, before riding a roller coaster or just prior to your entrance onstage. Setting a positive scene in your mind may channel your nervous energy to a higher score.

During your break, *stay away* from your fellow test-takers. You don't want to hear someone else's version of the right answer. ("I got –12 for that one! You didn't? Uh oh.") Test-chat won't help you and may increase your anxiety level. It's also against the rules.

Starting off

The test proctor distributes the booklets with, perhaps, a vindictive thump. (*Vindictive* means "seeking revenge," the sort of attitude that says, "Ha, ha! You're taking this awful test, and I'm not!") Before you get to the actual questions, the proctor instructs you how to fill in the top of the answer sheet with your name, date of birth, Social Security number, registration number, and so forth. Your admission ticket has the necessary information. You also have to copy some numbers from your test booklet onto the answer sheet. You must grid in all those numbers and letters. Filling in bubbles with a pencil is such a fun way to spend a weekend morning, don't you think?

Don't open the test booklet early. Big no-no! The proctor can send you home, scoreless and SAT-less, for starting early, working after time is called, or looking at the wrong section.

The proctor announces each section and tells you when to start and stop. The proctor probably uses the wall clock or his/her own wristwatch to time you. When the proctor says that you're starting at 9:08 and finishing at 9:33, take a moment to glance at the watch you brought. If you have a different time, reset your watch. Marching to a different drummer may be fun in real life, but not during the SAT.

Focusing during the test

Keep your eyes on your own paper, except for quick glimpses at your watch, so you can concentrate on the task at hand. If you glance around the room, you may see someone who has already finished. Then you'll panic: *Why is he done, and I'm only on Question 2?* You don't need this kind of idea rattling around in your head when you should be analyzing the author's tone in Passage III. Also, wandering eyes open you to a charge of cheating.

If your eye wants to run around sending signals to your brain like *I glimpsed Number 15, and it looks hard,* create a window of concentration. Place your hand over the questions you've already done and your answer sheet over the questions you haven't gotten to yet. Keep only one or two questions in eye-range. As you work, move your hand and the answer sheet, exposing only one or two questions at a time.

You aren't allowed to use scrap paper, but you *are* allowed to write all over the test booklet. If you eliminate a choice, put an *X* through it. If you think you've got two possible answers but aren't sure which is best, circle the ones you're considering. Then you can return to the question and take a guess.

If you skip a question, be careful to skip that line on your answer sheet. When you choose an answer, say (silently, to yourself), "The answer to Number 12 is (B)." Look at the answer sheet to be sure you're on Line 12, filling in the little oval for (B). Some people like to answer three questions at a time, writing the answers in the test booklet and *then* transferring them to the answer sheet. Not a bad idea! The answer sheet has alternating stripes of shaded and nonshaded ovals, three questions per stripe. The color helps you ensure that you're putting your answers in the correct spot. Take care not to run out of time, however. Nothing from your test booklet counts; only the answers you bubble in add to your score.

Pacing yourself

The SAT-makers do all kinds of statistical calculations to see which math questions stump most people and which are relatively simple. The test-makers place questions more or less in easy, medium, and hard order. The reading-comprehension and writing/language passages follow the order of the passage itself.

As you move through a section, you may find yourself feeling more and more challenged. When you approach the end, don't worry so much about skipping questions. You get the same amount of credit (one point) for each right answer from the "easy" portion of the test as you do for a correct response in the "hard" section. If you're stuck on an early question, take a guess, mark the question, and come back to it later. This way, you're sure to reach all the later questions that you're able to answer. Also, during the last minute of each section, bubble in an answer to every remaining question, perhaps choosing one letter and sticking with it for every blank. With no penalty for guessing, you may as well take a shot!

When you talk about easy and hard, one size doesn't fit all. A question that stumps 98 percent of the test-takers may be a no-brainer for you. Look at everything carefully. Don't assume that you can't answer a question at the end of a section; nor should you assume that you know everything in the beginning and panic if you don't.

Should you take the PSAT/NMSQT?

Complete this sentence: The PSAT/NMSQT is

(A) what you see on the bottom of the bowl when you don't eat all the alphabet soup

(B) the noise you make slurping the aforementioned soup

(C) a test that prepares you for the SAT and screens scholarship applicants

(D) a secret government agency that investigates music downloads from the Internet

The answer is Choice (C). The PSAT used to be short for the *Preliminary Scholastic Aptitude Test,* back when the initials SAT actually meant something. Now PSAT just means *Pre-SAT.* The NMSQT part still stands for something — *National Merit Scholarship Qualifying Test.* Though it has a two-part name, the PSAT/NMSQT is just one test, but it performs both the functions described in Choice (C). If you're a super brain, the PSAT/NMSQT may move you into the ranks of semifinalists for a National Merit Scholarship, a *prestigious* (high-status) scholarship program, or give you entry to other special programs. You don't have to do anything extra to apply for these scholarships and programs. Just take the test, and if you make the cut, the National Merit Scholarship Program and other organizations send you additional information. Some students who do not score high enough to become semifinalists will receive a Letter of Commendation, which also looks good on your college applications. Even if you think your chances of winning a scholarship or receiving a letter are the same as Bart Simpson's passing the fourth grade, you should still take the PSAT/NMSQT. The PSAT is changing along with the SAT and mirrors the SAT, though the PSAT is slightly shorter. Taking the PSAT gives you a feel for the SAT itself.

Chapter 3

Examining the Reading, Writing and Language, and Math Sections

In This Chapter

▶ Devising a strategy for reading passages

▶ Honing techniques for the writing and language questions and optional essay

▶ Maximizing your score on math problems

Two seconds after Ugh the Cave Dweller first carved some words on a rock wall, a prehistoric teacher-type (PT-T) asked, "What does 'Mastodon eat you' imply?" and the reading exam was born. When PT-T carved a correction ("Mastodon *eats* you"), the writing test began. And — you guessed it — the math exam came to life when PT-T commented, "Today you carved two words more than yesterday. At this rate of increase, how many will you carve tomorrow?"

Your test may be a bit tougher than Ugh's, but don't worry. In this chapter, you place each section and each type of question under a microscope and discover the best strategy for arriving at the correct answer.

Getting Acquainted with the Reading Section

The new SAT sends sentence completions — statements with blanks into which you insert an appropriate word — into *oblivion* (nonexistence). Instead, the SAT-makers have beefed-up the reading-comprehension passages, adding graphics and questions about evidence. In this way, the College Board attempts to relate 65 minutes of highly artificial reading to your ability to plow through 50 or 60 pounds of textbooks (or the electronic equivalent) each semester. Here's what you can expect:

✔ **Single passages:** You see four single passages on the test, each from 500 to 750 words long. Attached to each passage are 10 to 11 multiple-choice questions.

✔ **Paired passage:** One pair appears on every SAT Reading section. The total word count of the pair is 500 to 750 words. Most pairs offer two *distinct* (different) points of view on one issue. Either 10 or 11 questions come with each pair.

✔ **Content:** You get one passage drawn from a work of literature, two passages (or one passage and one pair) from history/social studies, and two passages (or one passage and one pair) from science.

✔ **Graphics:** You won't see a picture of the main character in a literary passage, but you will see charts, graphs, or diagrams similar to those that appear in textbooks. One or two will be attached to science passages and one or two to history passages.

✔ **Level:** The reading level of the passages ranges from ninth and tenth grade to just before college entry.

For information on types of questions and strategy, read on.

Conquering passage-based questions

When you enter SAT Reading-Passage World, be sure to take weapons — not swords and machine guns but logic and comprehension skills. This section shows you how to answer SAT reading questions, whether they're attached to single passages or pairs.

Speaking factually

It never hurts to have some real-world knowledge in your test-taking toolbox, but don't panic when you encounter a passage and several fact-based questions about a topic you've never heard of. The SAT reading questions never require you to know anything beyond what's presented in the passage. So even though you run when you see a bug, you can still master all the questions related to a passage about beetles and flies.

Cracking all types of passages

The new SAT consciously pulls passages from several subject areas and *genres* (types of writing). Check out these hints for approaching science, social studies/history, and literary passages.

When you're attacking a science passage, try these tactics:

✔ **Search out the facts.** Whatever the topic, a science passage offers information gained from experiments, surveys, or observation (or a combination of all three). Some of the information is in the text and some in the graphic, if the passage is illustrated. You don't need to know any math to answer a science-passage question, but you should pay close attention to numbers — percentages, populations, rates of growth or change, and so forth.

✔ **Don't worry about technical terms, but do know general science vocabulary.** If you see a strange word, the definition is probably tucked into the sentence. You won't encounter a question based on the definition of *Tephritidae* unless the passage explains what *Tephritidae* is (a type of fruit fly). Look for these definitions as you read. You should, however, know general terms that pop up frequently

in science-related material, such as *control group* (a group that doesn't participate in an experiment and serves as a point of comparison) and *catalyst* (a substance that causes or increases the rate of a chemical process without being affected itself). As you work through the practice exam in Chapter 4, notice the definitions in the answer explanations (in Chapter 7). Keep a list from your reading in science class, too.

✔ **Identify the argument.** Many science passages, and especially paired passages, present a dispute between two viewpoints. The SAT questions may zero in on the evidence for each scientific *theory* (a claim, backed up by evidence gained from experiments) or *hypothesis* (an idea to be tested through the scientific method) and then quiz you about each author's stance. By the way, remember the definitions of *theory* and *hypothesis,* two important science terms.

✔ **Notice the examples, both in print and in graphics.** The SAT science passages are chock-full of examples. The questions may require you to figure out what the examples prove.

If you're poring over a passage from history or social studies (anthropology, sociology, education, cultural studies, and so on), keep these tips in mind:

- ✔ **Go for the positive.** The SAT doesn't criticize anyone with the power to sue or contact the media. So if you see a question about the author's tone or viewpoint, look for a positive answer unless the passage is about war criminals or another crew unlikely to be met with public sympathy.

- ✔ **Take note of the structure.** The passages frequently present a claim and support it with sets of facts or quotations from experts. If you're asked about the significance of a particular detail in a passage, the detail is probably evidence in the case that the author is making. In a history passage, *chronology* (order of events) may be particularly important. Sketch a short timeline if the passage seems to focus on a series of linked events.

- ✔ **Check the graphics.** The information presented in tables, charts, diagrams, and other visuals is there for a reason. It may represent an opposing or *corroborative* (supporting or confirming) point.

- ✔ **Identify cause and effect.** History and social studies passages often explain *why* something happens. Search for words such as *therefore, hence, consequently,* and others that signal a reason.

- ✔ **Look for opposing ideas.** Experts like to argue, and human nature — the ultimate subject of social studies passages — provides plenty of arguable material. Historians, too, have been known to face off like opposing teams in a hockey game, criticizing others' interpretations of archaeological discoveries or important events. Many history/social studies SAT passages present two or more viewpoints, in the paired passages and elsewhere. Look for the opposing sides, or identify the main theory and the objections to it.

If you face a literary passage on the SAT (one from fiction or a memoir) keep in mind the following tips:

- ✔ **Notice the details.** SAT literary passages often contain a great deal of description, as in "George toppled the structure, which was made of stacked, square pancakes soaked in maple syrup." Take note of the small stuff, because you may find a question addressing the symbolism of *maple syrup* or *square pancakes*.

- ✔ **Stay attuned to word choice.** A literary passage is perfectly suited to questions about the author's tone (bitter, nostalgic, fond, critical, and so forth). Pay attention to *connotation* — not the dictionary definition but the feelings associated with a word.

- ✔ **Keep in mind the big picture.** Literary questions frequently single out one example and ask you to explain its context or significance. Think about the big picture when you get to one of these questions. How does the detail fit into the whole?

- ✔ **Forget about plot.** Plot isn't important in fiction passages because not much can happen in 500 or so words. Concentrate on identifying scene, character traits, point of view, and symbols.

- ✔ **Listen to a literary passage.** Of course, you can't make any noise while taking the SAT, but you can let the little voice in your head read expressively, as if you were acting. Chances are you'll pick up some information from your mental reenactment that you can use when answering the questions.

Fact-based questions zero in on statements in the passage. They test whether you comprehend the meaning of what you're actually reading. For example, in a descriptive paragraph, a fact-based question may ask whether the neighborhood is crowded or sparsely populated. In a science passage, you may be asked the result of an experiment.

Never skip a fact-based question because it's almost impossible to end up with a wrong answer. Amazingly enough, the test-makers often refer you to the very line in the passage that contains the answer.

SAT fact-based questions *do* have a couple of traps built in. Sometimes the test-writers word the passage in a confusing way. Successfully decoding a question's meaning depends on your ability to pick up the word clues embedded in the passage. Here are a few of the words SAT-makers love to use to keep you on your toes, and some explanations of what they really mean. (You may want to memorize these words so they're in neon lights in your brain.)

✔ **Except, but, not, in contrast to, otherwise, although, even though, despite, in spite of:** These words indicate contrast, identifying something that doesn't fit the pattern.

✔ **And, also, in addition to, as well as, moreover, furthermore, not only . . . but also, likewise, not the only:** When you see these clue words, you're probably looking for something that does fit the pattern.

✔ **Therefore, because, consequently, hence, thus, accordingly, as a result:** Now you're in cause-and-effect land. Look for something that causes or leads to something else (or something caused by something else).

✔ **Than, like, equally, similarly:** Time to compare two ideas, two quantities, two people, two actions — you get the idea.

✔ **Until, after, later, then, once, before, since, while, during, still, yet, earlier, finally, when:** You're watching the clock (or calendar) when you see these clue words. Think about the order of events.

Time for a sample question, based on this excerpt from a science passage about an unusual animal.

Line As a rule the dancing mouse is considerably smaller than the common mouse. All the dancing mice have black eyes and are smaller as well as weaker than the common gray house mouse. The weakness, indicated by their inability to hold up their own weight or to cling to an object, curiously enough does not manifest itself in their dancing; in this they are (05) tireless. Frequently they run in circles or whirl about with astonishing rapidity for several minutes at a time.

According to the passage, in what way is a dancing mouse superior to other types of mice?

(A) endurance

(B) muscle strength

(C) ability to cling

(D) weight

Line 5 tells you that the dancing mouse is "tireless," so Choice (A) is a good bet. Before you settle there, test the other choices. The passage tells you that these mice are "smaller as well as weaker" (Line 2), so you can rule out Choices (B) and (D). Because dancing mice are unable "to cling to an object" (Line 4), Choice (C) is wrong. You're left with Choice (A), the right answer.

Clue words show up in the questions, too, so be *vigilant* (on your guard) when reading the questions, not just while perusing the reading passage itself.

Defining as you read

Many SAT questions ask you to define a word as it's used in the passage. Teacher-types call this exercise *vocabulary in context*. Never skip a vocabulary-in-context question because sometimes the definition is actually in the same sentence. Even if the definition is missing, figuring out the meaning of the word is usually easy. Consider what the sentence or paragraph as a whole is saying. Insert a logical word or phrase of your own choice in place of the word they're asking about. Match your word with an answer choice, and you're done. Here's an example, based on the "dancing mouse" passage in the preceding section.

In Line 4, the best definition of "manifest" is

(A) emphasize

(B) prove

(C) discover

(D) show

Line 4 tells you that the weakness of dancing mice "does not manifest itself in their dancing." Mentally, cross out *manifest* and throw in a possible replacement. The passage tells you that the mice can "dance" rapidly for several minutes at a time. That activity isn't weak. Okay, the activity doesn't *show* weakness, a match for Choice (D), which is your answer.

Vocabulary-in-context questions do contain one big sand trap, though. Many of these questions ask you for the definition of a word you probably already know. But — and this is a big *but* — the passage may use the word in an odd or unusual way. Of course, one of the choices is usually the word's definition that you know, just sitting there waiting for the unwary test-taker to grab it. For example, the word *deck* may mean "a surface of a ship," "a wooden structure outside a house," or "to decorate." In the Christmas carol, "Deck the Halls," *deck* matches the last meaning. Don't settle for *any* definition of the vocabulary word. Look for the definition that works in the context of the sentence.

Identifying attitude and tone

An *attitude* in a reading passage goes way beyond the "don't take that attitude [or tone] with me" comment that parents repeat with depressing regularity. In SAT jargon, an attitude or tone can be critical, objective, indifferent, and so forth. The following clue words may pop up in the answer choices:

- **Pro, positive, in favor of, leaning toward, *laudatory* (praising), agreeable, *amenable* (willing to go along with), sympathetic:** The author is *for* a particular topic or argument.

- **Doubtful, offended, anti, resistant to, contrary to, counter to, *adversarial* (acting like an enemy), opposed, skeptical, critical of, disgusted with:** The author is *against* a particular topic or argument.

- **Objective, indifferent, noncommittal, impartial, *apathetic* (not caring), unbiased, *ambivalent* (can't decide either way or has mixed feelings):** The author is *neutral* on a particular topic or argument.

To answer an attitude question, first decide where the author lands — for, against, or neutral — in relation to the topic. Check for clue words that express approval or disapproval.

A variation of the attitude question asks you to identify the author's *tone.* Tone and attitude overlap a little, but tone is closer to what you'd hear if the passage were the words of someone speaking directly to you. You can use most of the same clues you use for attitude to help you figure out the author's tone. Just remember that tone questions include emotions, so check for irony, amusement, nostalgia, regret, and sarcasm.

In paired passages, you often run into questions comparing tone or attitude, such as

> In comparison with Passage I, Passage II is more . . .

> The author of Passage II would probably agree with the author of Passage I regarding . . .

To answer such a question, determine the tone or attitude separately and then compare the two. Be sure to read the question stem (the part preceding the multiple-choice answers) especially carefully. Words such as *more* or *less* really matter in comparisons!

Take a crack at this attitude question, based on an excerpt from a story by Virginia Woolf.

Line "Fifteen years ago I came here with Lily," he thought. "We sat somewhere over there by a lake and I begged her to marry me all through the hot afternoon. How the dragonfly kept circling round us: how clearly I see the dragonfly and her shoe with the square silver buckle at the toe. All the time I spoke I saw her shoe and when it moved impatiently I knew without (05) looking up what she was going to say: the whole of her seemed to be in her shoe. And my love, my desire, were in the dragonfly; for some reason I thought that if it settled there, on that leaf, she would say 'Yes' at once. But the dragonfly went round and round: it never settled anywhere — of course not, happily not, or I shouldn't be walking here with Eleanor and the children."

In this passage, the speaker's attitude may best be characterized as

(A) mocking

(B) confused

(C) nostalgic

(D) argumentative

In this paragraph, the speaker looks at the past, remembering an afternoon when he "begged" (Line 2) a woman to accept his marriage proposal. He's *nostalgic* (feeling pleasure and yearning for something in the past) so Choice (C) is correct. The yearning, which contains a hint of sadness, shows in Lily's refusal, which he now sees "happily" (Line 8).

Decoding figurative language

Appearances often deceive on the SAT. The passage may contain one or more symbols, similes, or metaphors (all types of *figurative* language) that have a deeper meaning.

Questions about figurative language may resemble the following:

> ✔ In the second paragraph, the author compares _____ to _____ because . . .
>
> ✔ The _____ mentioned in Line 8 symbolizes . . .

The best strategy for answering symbol- or metaphor-based questions is to form a picture in your brain. Try your hand at a figurative language question, based on the Virginia Woolf excerpt in the preceding section:

In this passage, Lily's shoe most likely represents

(A) Lily's desire to protect others

(B) Lily's reluctance to settle down

(C) Lily's love for the narrator

(D) the narrator's attraction to Lily

Line 4 tells you that Lily's shoe "moved impatiently." The narrator sees the dragonfly and the shoe together and notes that the dragonfly "never settled anywhere" (Lines 7 and 8). The shoe and Lily's mood are clearly related, so Choice (B) is the right answer here.

Relating style to content

An increasing number of questions on the redesigned SAT ask you to examine *how* a particular passage is written and *why* the author wrote it that way — in other words, to relate style to content or purpose. Here are a few examples:

> ✔ The statistics about fish consumption demonstrate that . . .
>
> ✔ The marine biologist's quoted statement that the fishing should be regulated (Line 4) serves to . . .
>
> ✔ The description of the marine ecosystem exemplifies . . .

The key to this sort of question is to get inside the writer's mind. "Why did the author put that particular example or quotation in that particular place?" The example may be a small detail in a paragraph full of details. If so, try to decide what title you'd give to the paragraph. Depending on the paragraph's contents, you may choose "Why we should stop catching cod" or "The ocean is overrun with cod" as a good title for the list. After you get the title, you should be able to choose the answer choice that best explains why the writer chose to use the example in the passage. Alternatively, the example may be one complete paragraph out of many in the passage. In that case, what title would you give this passage? Chances are giving the passage a fitting title can lead you to the correct response.

Style and content often show up in paired-passage questions, because two authors may make the same point in completely different ways. To answer a question like this, determine the style and content separately, place your conclusions side by side, and notice the similarities and differences. Chances are one of the answer choices will match your ideas. If not, move on unless you have a lot of extra time. This sort of question requires close reading, and you may do better by concentrating on an easier and less time-consuming question.

Try your hand at this style question, based on a history passage describing settlers traveling to the West during the 19th century:

Line During all this time, and despite the disagreeable weather, emigrants from the cities of the Northeast to the wilderness in the West keep up the line of march, traveling in their "prairie schooners," as the great hoop-covered wagon is called, into which, often are packed their every worldly possession, and have room to pile in a large family on top. Sometimes a
(05) sheet-iron stove is carried along at the rear of the wagon, which, when needed, they set up inside and put the pipe through a hole in the covering. Those who do not have this convenience carry wood with them and build a fire on the ground to cook by; cooking utensils are generally packed in a box at the side or front. The coverings of the wagons are of all shades and materials. When oil cloth is not used, they are often patched over the top with their
(10) oil-cloth table covers, saving them from the rain.

The details about the wagon serve to

(A) reveal the convenience of covered wagons

(B) emphasize the ingenuity of the travelers

(C) show that the travelers were ill-equipped for life on the frontier

(D) contrast life in the city with life in the wilderness

Why does the author describe the covered wagons in so much detail? Probably to tell you something about the travelers themselves. They seem clever (and *ingenuity* means "cleverness"): They pack everything they need into one wagon. Some have more than others, but those who, for example, lack stoves, "carry wood and build a fire on the ground" (Line 7). They protect themselves from the rain with either a wagon cover or a tablecloth. Did you fall for Choices (C) or (D)? You don't learn much about the land they're traveling through, except that the weather isn't great. Plus, the passage doesn't give any hints about the final destination or the travelers' previous situations. So Choice (B) is best.

Unearthing the main idea

In reading terms, the questions on the SAT that address the main idea of a particular passage give you choices that fall into the too-broad, too-narrow, off-base, or just-right categories. A just-right choice includes all the supporting points and details in the passage, but it isn't so broad as to be meaningless.

Imagine for a moment that you're trying to find a main idea for a list that includes the following: jelly, milk, waxed paper, light bulbs, and peaches. A main idea that fits is *things you can buy at the supermarket.* One that is too broad is *stuff.* A too-narrow choice is *food,* because very few people like the taste of light bulbs — and everyone who does is locked up in a padded room somewhere. A completely off-base main idea is *canned goods.*

Look back at the paragraph about covered wagons in the preceding section to answer this question.

Which of the following titles best fits the main idea of this passage?

(A) Cooking on the Frontier

(B) A Pioneering People

(C) Prairie Schooners

(D) Wilderness Encounters

The paragraph describes covered wagons, also known as "prairie schooners," according to Lines 2 and 3. Therefore, Choice (C) is perfect. Choice (A) is too narrow, and Choice (B) is too broad. Choice (D) is off topic, because no one *encounters* anyone else in this passage.

Making inferences

You make inferences every day. (An *inference* is a conclusion you reach based on evidence.) Perhaps you come home and your mother is chewing on the phone bill and throwing your bowling trophies out the window. Even though she hasn't stated the problem, you can guess that the call you made to the bowling team in Helsinki wasn't included in your basic monthly calling plan.

The SAT Reading section features many inference questions. You get a certain amount of information, and then you have to stretch it a little. The questions may resemble the following:

✔ What may be inferred from the author's statement that "further study should include archaeological digs" (Line 66)?

✔ The author implies in Line 12 that the documents were . . .

✔ The author would probably agree with which of the following statements?

To crack an inference question, you've got to act like Sherlock Holmes. You have a few clues, perhaps some statements about historical documents: No one has decoded the writing system from that era. One document is missing key pages. The authors of that culture gave equal weight to mythological and governmental accounts. You get the picture? Then ask yourself what sort of conclusion you can come to, given the evidence. You may decide that the author recommends archaeological investigation because he or she sees what's lacking in other sorts of historical records. After you reach a conclusion, check the answer choices for one that matches your idea.

If you're asked to infer, don't look for a statement that's actually in the passage. By definition, inferences reside between the lines. If you think you found a direct statement in the passage, it's the wrong answer.

Try your hand at this inference question, based on these sentences about the westward journey of settlers during the 19th century.

The women generally do the driving, while the men and boys bring up the rear with horses and cattle of all grades, from poor weak calves to fine fat animals, that show they have had a good living where they came from.

With which statement would the travelers described in this passage probably agree?

(A) Gender distinctions are valid considerations in assigning work.

(B) All livestock should be treated equally.

(C) Only healthy animals can survive a long journey.

(D) Many pioneers are motivated by greed.

The passage tells you that women drive while "men and boys" are in the rear with "horses and cattle." Clearly, gender plays a part in assigning work, so Choice (A) is the correct answer.

Supplying evidence

Two questions out of every set of 10 to 11 reading questions ask you to identify evidence for your answer. The wording will resemble this:

> Which lines support the answer to the preceding question?

These questions are so easy, they're practically freebies! Unless you're guessing, you always select an answer for a reason. All you have to do to answer an evidence question is to (1) get the answer to the first question right, and (2) find an answer choice that matches the *reason* you selected your answer to the first question. To see this technique in action, read the explanations accompanying the answers to every sample reading question in this chapter. See the lines and words cited as evidence? Those lines may form the answer to an evidence question.

Interpreting visual elements

Bowing to the real world, where visual elements — charts, tables, graphs, diagrams, and so forth — carry valuable information, the redesigned SAT includes visuals in science and history/social studies passages. (The new SAT Writing and Language and Mathematics sections have visuals, too; check out the "Writing for (No) Fun and Much Profit" and "Refreshing the Math" sections, later in this chapter, for more information.) To *garner* (harvest) every scrap of information from a visual element, follow these guidelines:

- **Look at everything.** The title, the explanation on the top, bottom, or sides, the labels inside a diagram — *everything.* You never know which part may be relevant. Imagine the difference in a graph with bars reaching levels of 12, 18, and 11. Now imagine that you neglected to read the note telling you that each level represented 10,000 people. A bar drawn to level 12, then, represents not a dozen people but 120,000 — a fact you can be sure the SAT-makers will quiz you on.

- **Note all the variables.** Depending on the type of graph you see, a *variable* (what changes) may be represented by a line, a section of a circle, or a bar. Some graphs include more than one factor — perhaps a solid line *depicting* (showing) peanut butter sales and a dotted line tracing jelly sales. Bars may appear in pairs, with one a deep shade and the other a little lighter, comparing peanut butter and jelly sales each year. You need all the information you can get to answer some questions.

- **Note the relationship between the visual element and the text.** Most of the time, these two parts work together. The imaginary bar graph referred to in the preceding bullet point may tell you how many people took the SAT in a particular year, while the text may explain how many test-takers sat for the SAT in a particular geographical area. Together, these statistics may help you answer a question about — well, SAT distribution, testing misery, or something else.

Visual elements are good sources for fact or inference questions. Try this one.

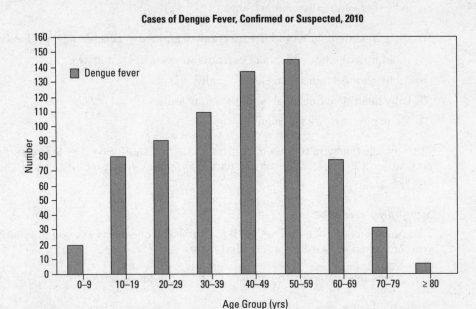

Cases of Dengue Fever, Confirmed or Suspected, 2010

Source: Centers for Disease Control, U.S. Government.

Which statement about Dengue Fever is true?

(A) Infants are less likely to contract Dengue Fever than the elderly.

(B) In 2010, most cases of Dengue Fever occurred in people aged 40 to 60.

(C) The risk of catching Dengue Fever rises with age.

(D) Dengue Fever is especially dangerous for infants and children.

The bar graph shows the number of cases of Dengue Fever, not the danger. A glance at the height of each bar tells the rest of the story: The bars for ages 40 to 49 and 50 to 59 are higher than those for other age groups. Therefore, Choice (B) is correct.

Making the Most of Your Time

When you're barreling through the Reading section on the SAT, time is your *foe* (enemy). To maximize your score, you need to concentrate on questions you're fairly certain you can answer correctly. In general, follow these steps (and refer to the preceding sections for question-specific details):

1. **Answer the factual questions.**

   These questions are usually straightforward, and the question usually supplies a line number so you know where to look for the answer.

2. **Go to the vocabulary-in-context type of question.**

   These questions generally rely on your understanding of only one or two sentences and can be answered quickly.

3. **Answer all evidence questions.**

   This is a two-for-the-price-of-one deal. Unless the question preceding the evidence question stumped you, *never* skip an evidence question.

4. **If time is running out, skip questions that ask you to interpret the author's tone or attitude or to identify the main idea.**

   These questions rely on a solid understanding of the entire passage. If anything is unclear and you don't have time to reread, move on to other questions.

5. **If the test-makers ask questions about relationships between paragraphs, style, inferences, and visual elements, do the ones that seem obvious to you and skip the rest.**

   Go back if you have time for the tough ones.

6. **In paired passages, work on each passage separately and then on questions about the pair.**

   Answer all the Passage I questions that you know immediately and then all the Passage II questions that you can ace with no trouble. Then tackle the shared-passage queries.

7. **In the last minute, bubble at random or finish one last question properly.**

   If you have a chance to mull over a question and achieve a correct answer, do so. If not, bubble everything you omitted, choosing a letter that you like (A for your grade? B for your best friend?).

No matter which questions you answer first, remember one important rule: You get as many points for a correct answer to an easy question as you do for a correct answer to a hard question. Nope, it's not fair. But then again, this is the SAT. Fairness *isn't* part of the deal.

Deciding Which to Read First: Passage or Questions

Potential SAT-takers often wonder whether they should read the passage or the questions first. A variation of this query is whether to read the passages at all. The answer to the second question is easy: Never skip the passage. Ever. As for which to read first, make the decision based on your personal style. Are you good at keeping details in your head? If so, go for the read-the-question-first option. Don't read all the choices; just glance at the *tag line* (the beginning of the question) so you have a rough idea of what the testers want to know.

If you feel that your head is filled with too many facts already, settle in with the passage before you look at the questions. Keep your pencil handy and circle anything that looks particularly important. Write a word next to each paragraph, summing up its main idea ("hot dog line," "argument for the designated hitter," and so on). Then hit the questions and locate the answers. Many students who ace the SAT take marginal notes during the test, so give it a try!

Whether you read the passage or question first, never skip the italicized introduction to a passage. Many SAT passages are preceded by a short italicized description along the lines of *this passage comes from the diary of a 16th-century maniac* or *the author of this passage was locked in an SAT test site for 14 days before being rescued.* This description orients you to the passage and may help you decide the author's tone or attitude. You won't see a factual question based on the italicized introduction, but you may be sure that the SAT doesn't waste words, and whatever the test-writers say in italics is useful in some way.

Writing for (No) Fun but Much Profit: The SAT Writing and Language Section

What's "trending" on the new SAT? Out of the picture are questions based on random single sentences — the old "error recognition" and "sentence improvement" questions. The redesigned SAT Writing and Language section attaches multiple-choice questions to short passages, so your revisions have a context. The SAT Writing and Language section still features an essay, but the redesigned SAT essay doesn't ask — or care about — your opinion on a topic, as the old essay did. Instead, you may write an essay based on a passage, analyzing the writer's style choices. The essay is also optional, not required as it was on the older test.

Whether you're headed for the Nobel Prize in Literature or ideas expressed only with emoticons (those little drawings that take the place of words), you still have to conquer the Writing and Language section of the SAT. To score big, read on.

Multiple-choice writing and language questions

The new SAT design most closely resembles the passage-improvement questions on the old exam. Instead of six multiple-choice, passage-improvement questions, though, the new SAT hits you with 44 questions that you must answer in 35 minutes. Here are the details:

- Each passage is 400 to 450 words long.

- You see one passage in each of these categories: science, history/social studies, careers, and humanities (writing about literature, art, and the like).

- One or two passages make an argument, one or two give information, and one narrates a series of events.

- Graphics (tables, charts, diagrams, and so forth) appear with one or more passages.

- Eleven questions are attached to each passage. Twenty questions cover Standard English conventions — better known as grammar and punctuation. An additional 24 questions address style, what the College Board calls "Expression of Ideas." This last category is broad and may include word choice (selecting the right word for a particular context), concise writing, organization, logic, and effective use of evidence.

- The complexity of language and graphics ranges from ninth to tenth grade through post-high-school level.

Passage-based questions are relatively easy, if you approach them in the right way. The following sections present the best strategy for the most common types of questions.

Selecting the right word: Vocabulary in context

No section of the SAT tests vocabulary directly, but every section checks whether you grasp the *nuances* (shades of meaning) of an expression in a particular context. In the Writing and Language section, one word — usually a fairly sophisticated word — appears where it may not quite fit. The answer choices appear in the margin without a question stem. They offer alternatives. These questions arise from the fact that English is rich in word choices, many with nearly the same meaning. Nearly, though, isn't good enough when you're writing. For instance, your eyelids don't *tremble* when you're flirting; they *flutter*. Both words refer to quick, small movements, but only one is appropriate for a sentence about attracting a romantic partner.

The best long-term preparation for word-use questions is reading. When you read, you probably run across unfamiliar words. Make a note of every new word, along with the sentence or phrase the words appears in. The context helps you remember the meaning and gives you a head start in *deciphering* (figuring out) vocabulary questions.

To answer a vocabulary-in-context question on the Writing and Language section, be sure you know both the definition and the *connotation* (feelings or situations associated with the word). Time for you to try one, which is *embedded* (implanted, set in firmly) in a sentence that would be part of a longer passage:

Few in the community are pleased with the plan to construct a sewage plant on First Street. Opponents <u>detract</u> the proposed facility despite claims that it will bring much-needed jobs to the area.

How should the underlined word be changed, if at all?

(A) NO CHANGE

(B) criticize

(C) degrade

(D) diminish

To detract is "to take value away from," a definition that is related to criticism but not exactly the same. Orange sequins may *detract from* the elegant outfit you're trying to assemble, and if you wear them, someone may *criticize* you, but no one will *detract* you. Go for Choice (B). By the way, *to degrade* is "to treat with disrespect," as in "an advertisement that degrades women" and *to diminish* is "to lessen in value or amount," as in "his appetite diminished after he saw what the chef had prepared."

Correcting grammar and punctuation errors

Even if you've always wanted to tear a grammar book into tiny little pieces, you can still do well on grammar and punctuation questions. The new SAT concentrates on the most important *principles* (rules) of Standard English — the way educated people speak and write. You see a word or phrase underlined and have to determine whether a change is needed. (The same format shows up in style questions.) Here are some guidelines for grammar and punctuation questions in SAT Writing and Language passages:

- ✔ **Keep an eye open for incorrect punctuation.** Always check apostrophes and commas. Apostrophes may show up in possessive pronouns, such as *theirs* (where they don't belong), or they may be missing in contractions, such as *don't* and *won't* (where they're needed). Many passages and answer choices contain comma splices, two complete sentences incorrectly combined with a comma rather than a semicolon or a *conjunction — and, but, because,* and similar words. You may see, for example, a "sentence" like this one: "George robbed a bank, consequently, he went to jail." The comma after *bank* should be replaced by a period.

- ✔ **Be sure every sentence is complete.** Comma splices (see the preceding bullet point) and *fragments* (half sentences such as "Although it is raining and the picnic is canceled") are incorrect in Standard English. Look for an alternative that inserts a semicolon (;) or a conjunction (*and, because,* and similar words).

- ✔ **Don't worry about spelling and capitalization mistakes.** The SAT doesn't test spelling, and very infrequently takes on capitalization. Assume that capital letters are in the right spots unless a glaring mistake jumps out at you.

- ✔ **Watch out for verbs.** Verb tense is a big deal on the SAT, as is subject-verb agreement (choosing a singular or plural verb to match a singular or plural subject). When you check the subject-verb pair, ignore interrupters — descriptions, for example, that show up between a subject and its matching verb. For example, you may come across a sentence like this one: "The toddler, along with seven friends and their nannies, have gone to the playground." In this sentence the verb *have* should be replaced by *has,* as the subject of the sentence is *toddler.*

✔ **Pay attention to pronouns.** The SAT-writers often mix singular and plural forms incorrectly, such as matching the singular noun *person* with the plural pronoun *they.* Also check pronoun *case* — be sure that an object pronoun such as *him* functions as an object in the sentence, a subjevct pronoun such as *he* is a subject, and so forth. Take a look at this example: "Mary asked that we keep the discussion between you and I." In this sentence, the pronoun *I* is incorrect, because you need an object pronoun, *me,* after the preposition *between.*

✔ **Notice parallel structure.** In English-teacher terminology, *parallel* structure means that everything doing the same job in the sentence must have the same grammatical identity. For example, you can enjoy *surfing, skiing, and hiking,* but not *surfing, skiing, and to hike.* Check for parallelism in lists and comparisons. Also pay attention to parallelism when ideas are combined with *either/or, neither/nor, not only/but also, both/and, as/as,* and similar conjunction pairs. Whatever these pairs join must be parallel.

✔ **Check the placement of descriptions.** No matter how long or short, a description must be close to the word it describes. Every description must be clearly attached to one word, and only one word. No *ambiguity* (having more than one interpretation) is allowed.

If you locate a grammar or punctuation mistake, be sure that your answer choice doesn't contain a *different* error. You must be able to plug in the new version and end up with a proper sentence.

Ready to practice? Try this sample question, excerpted from a science passage.

Samples taken every quarter mile along the river show the extent of the problem. The water five miles downstream <u>not only was polluted but also laden with debris</u>, including tires, chunks of wood, and plastic trash bags.

How should the underlined words be changed, if at all?

(A) NO CHANGE

(B) was not only polluted but also laden with debris

(C) not only polluted but also debris was laden there

(D) not only polluted but also laden with debris

The paired conjunction *not only/but also* should trigger an immediate check for parallelism. After *not only*, you have a verb, *was.* After *but also,* you don't have a verb. Choice (D) removes the verb, but now you're left with a "sentence" lacking a verb — not a sentence at all! Choice (B) moves the verb. Now *not only* and its partner *but also* join parallel elements — two descriptions, *polluted* and *laden.*

Note: This chapter deals with strategy for grammar and punctuation issues. If you need a full-scale grammar course, take a look at *English Grammar For Dummies,* 2nd Edition, *English Grammar Workbook For Dummies,* 2nd Edition, or *1,001 Grammar Practice Questions For Dummies,* all published by Wiley.

Answering "Expression of Ideas" questions

The College Board places style, logic, and organization questions in the "Expression of Ideas" category. As with grammar and punctuation questions, you may see an underlined word, phrase, or sentence and must determine whether it's the best possible way to express the idea. You may also be asked whether additional evidence is needed to support a point or whether a sentence should be deleted or moved to maintain focus. At least a couple of questions relate to the visual element.

When you approach a question in the "Expression of Ideas" category, keep these points in mind:

✔ **Underlined material may be grammatically correct but wordy or awkward.** The answer choices may include a more mature or fluid version.

✔ **Briefer is usually better.** It takes a long time to learn to write *concisely* (with few words), and the SAT tries to *distinguish* (recognize the difference between) whether you're a mature writer or a beginner. If you can cut repetitive words from the sentence *without* creating a grammar mistake, go for it!

✔ **Unity is crucial.** Everything in a paragraph should revolve around one idea. If a sentence hops off topic, it has to go.

✔ **The flow of logic is essential.** Check for smooth transitions between one paragraph and another. The reader should immediately realize why the writer moved in a particular direction. If not, identify what's missing in the answer choices.

✔ **Interpret visual information correctly.** The text may refer to the information that a chart, graph, or diagram contains. Be sure that the text says the same thing as the graphic element. If not, look for an answer choice that does.

✔ **Arguments need evidence.** If the passage puts forth a point of view, supporting facts or quotations should appear. Look for these additions in the answer choices if the original is lacking.

When you work on the Writing and Language multiple-choice questions, pretend that you wrote the piece. Ask yourself how you'd make it better. Then find the answer choice that fits your revision plan.

The essay

The new SAT features only one question that requires you to place words on paper — the essay — and that question is optional. You can add 50 minutes to the end of your SAT morning by writing the essay, which is the last section of the exam, or you can go home. By the way, most likely the words really will go on paper. The College Board is slowly — very slowly! — implementing computer-based testing, but the vast majority of test-takers will work without a screen or keyboard.

If you generally do well on in-class writing assignments, you should probably take a crack at the SAT essay. If you freeze when you're given a timed essay, consider opting out. Check with your English teacher, if you have one who knows you fairly well, for advice. Also check with colleges that are your top choices. Will they look at your essay score? Many admissions officers saw the old SAT essay as a waste of time because it asked test-takers simply to take a position on a random topic. Some SAT-takers wrote and memorized essays in advance, filled with "evidence" they'd made up to fit their views, and then transcribed the previously written work onto the answer sheet. The graders weren't permitted to downgrade the essay score because of obvious factual errors. The new essay section may be more popular with admissions offices because it's passage-based.

Every essay on the redesigned SAT has the same *prompt,* or question, which you can study in advance. The only variable is the passage, 650 to 750 words that make an argument for a particular point of view. In this section, you take a close look at the standard prompt and then find guidelines for the best approach to analyzing the passage. This section also explains an efficient and effective process for writing an essay expressing your ideas.

Decoding the prompt

The prompt you see when you take the SAT will resemble the following, with the real name of the writer taking the place of "Author" and briefly summarizing the author's point in the blank:

> As you read the passage, consider how Author uses the following:
>
> - Evidence such as facts or examples to support Author's ideas
>
> - Logic to develop the argument and link claims and supporting evidence
>
> - Style choices — appeals to emotion, figurative language, word choice, and so forth — to add to the persuasive power of the argument
>
> Write an essay in which you explain how Author constructs an argument to persuade the reader that _____. In your essay, discuss how Author uses one or more of the elements of style listed above, or other elements, to strengthen the logic and persuasiveness of Author's argument. Focus on the most important features of the passage. Do not explain whether you agree or disagree with Author's ideas. Instead, concentrate on how Author builds a persuasive case.

To summarize: The prompt tells you that your job is to analyze the author's argument and, most important, to discuss the writing techniques the author employs to convince readers of his or her point of view.

The prompt mentions a couple of possible writing techniques. Use those as a starting point, but don't limit yourself. If you notice a technique that isn't listed, go for it!

Identifying writing techniques

Every passage is different, but many techniques appear frequently when the author makes an argument. Here are several things to look for:

✔ **Logos, ethos, and pathos:** These Greek terms refer to general strategies for argument:

- *Logos* is an appeal to logic or reason. Factual evidence and examples may be part of logos. Perhaps the writer cites statistics on the rate of car crashes when the speed limit is lowered and refers to accident rates in neighboring areas with different traffic laws.

- *Ethos* relies on the character and qualifications of the writer (perhaps a highway patrol officer who regularly handled crash sites) or, in some cases, quotations from experts (perhaps urban planners). Look for references to authorities on the subject if you suspect that the writer is relying on *ethos* to make a point.

- *Pathos* hits the emotions. The writer may present a story about one particular accident victim, hoping to tug the readers' heartstrings.

✔ **Diction:** Word choice, or *diction,* may have a huge effect on the reader's reaction. Consider the difference between *privacy* and *loneliness* in an essay about solitude. One of those words (privacy) creates a positive impression, and the other (loneliness), a negative. Sophisticated vocabulary tells you that the writer sees the reader as educated and aware; simpler diction may create a "just us folks" impression of innocence.

✔ **Concession and reply:** Useful in written arguments (not to mention personal quarrels), this writing technique acknowledges and responds to the opposing point of view. Using the speed-limit example mentioned in the first bullet point, the author may concede that driver inattention has more influence on the accident rate than speed limits do but argue that lower speed limits save *some* lives and are therefore still desirable.

✔ **Structure:** The passage may be set up as a comparison (accident rates in Germany and in the United States), as cause-and-effect (the law was passed, and traffic fatalities dropped), or observations and conclusions (seemingly random facts that gradually forge a chain of logic), drawing the reader to the writer's point of view. As you read, try to *discern* (detect, perceive) the organizing principle of the passage.

✔ **Repetition and parallel structure:** A section of the Declaration of Independence lists the actions of King George III that the colonists object to. The writers use the expression "he has" more than 20 times. Normally, writers avoid repetition and a string of similar sentence patterns. In this document, however, the result is almost a criminal *indictment* (formal charge of wrongdoing). Each time you read "he has," the writers' case becomes stronger. As you read the passage, notice these elements. They may not appear, or you may see only two or three similar statements or words, arranged in parallel structure. (Parallelism is the English-teacher term for elements in a sentence that perform the same function and have the same grammatical identity. Don't worry about the terminology. Just notice patterns.) When you find repetition or parallelism, ask yourself why the writer chose this technique — to emphasize, to equate one item with another, or for another purpose.

✔ **Figurative language:** Imaginative comparisons, even in nonfiction passages, add depth to the writer's arguments. In his magnificent "I Have a Dream" speech, Martin Luther King Jr. refers to "the bank of justice" and a check returned from the bank marked "insufficient funds" to show the unmet demands for equal rights. These *metaphors* (comparisons made without the words *like* or *as*) relate King's argument for equality to a situation everyone with a bank account can understand. If you run across metaphors or other types of figurative language such as *similes* (comparisons made with *like* or *as*) or *personification* (giving human qualities to abstract or nonhuman elements), think about their effect on the reader.

Preparing, writing, and proofing the essay

Fifty minutes may seem like a lot, but those minutes fly by at the speed of light when you're writing. However, no matter how pressed for time you feel, your score will rise if you spend a few minutes (five to seven) preparing *before* you write the essay and another few minutes (or five to six) proofreading your work *after* you've written it. All the minutes in between are for the writing itself. Here's more detail on how to approach the essay:

1. **Read the passage, annotating as you go.**

   The *annotations* (notes or marks) should be very brief — an important feature underlined or circled, a word or abbreviation in the margin (for example, "sent struc" where you notice something interesting about *sentence structure* or "wc" when *word choice* matters).

2. **Be sure you understand the author's argument.**

   The second part of the prompt summarizes the author's position very briefly. Let that statement guide you, but before you write, *amplify* (expand) a little. Suppose the prompt says that the author favors lower speed limits, for example. Ask yourself *why*. The amplified version may be that the author favors lower speed limits on roads also used by cyclists and pedestrians or in limited-visibility conditions. If you grasp exactly what the writer believes, you have a better chance of understanding how the writer tries to convince the reader.

3. **Quickly decide which points are most important.**

   Fifty minutes isn't a lot, so you may not have time to write about everything you notice. Don't agonize. Select the most relevant points and move to the next step.

4. **Choose a structure.**

   The simplest structure follows the passage; you discuss the writing techniques you see in the passage in the order in which they appear, first discussing something in paragraph one, then paragraph two, and so on. A little more complicated but also more mature tactic is to group similar elements. You may have a paragraph about diction, for instance, analyzing the author's choice of words throughout the passage. Next up, perhaps, is a paragraph about the author's reliance on expert opinions *conveyed* (communicated) through quotations.

5. **Make an outline.**

   You don't have time for a formal outline, complete with roman numerals and fancy indentations. Jot down the points you'll make and letter them *A, B, C,* and so on.

6. **Write the essay.**

   Sounds easy, right? It isn't. But as one sneaker company says, "Just do it." As you write, take care to analyze, not just list. The graders give you little credit for saying that a simile appears in paragraphs two, four, and eight. They give you much more credit for explaining the effect of those similes on the reader. Also, avoid general statements, such as "This essay contains a lot of similes." Instead, quote the similes as you discuss them. Every point you make about the passage should be firmly attached to the text of the passage, either through a quotation or a specific reference ("the anecdote about the snake in paragraph two . . .").

7. **Proofread.**

   Look for misspelled words, awkward sentences, grammar mistakes, and the like. Correct your mistakes by crossing them out *neatly* (one line is enough) and inserting the proper word or punctuation.

When you proofread, you may think of a great addition to your essay. With limited space and time, you can't rewrite. So place your new idea at the end. Label it "insert A." Then make a note ("see insert A") at the spot in the essay where this point logically belongs.

Understanding your essay scores

The College Board, as of this moment, is still fine-tuning the essay question and may continue to do so even after the first couple of "new" SATs have been given. Current plans call for two readers, both awarding 1 to 4 points in each of these categories: reading (understanding what the writer says, including both the main idea and details), analysis (picking apart the writing techniques), and writing (expressing your ideas). More specifically, the graders check these skills:

- ✓ **Reading:** Comprehending the main idea of the passage, noting details and their relationship to the main idea, grasping the structure of the passage

- ✓ **Analysis:** Evaluating the author's use of evidence, logic, and persuasive techniques

- ✓ **Writing:** Supporting your statements in a well-organized essay that employs evidence (quotations or paraphrased examples) and shows mature writing style (varied sentence patterns, consistent tone, and grammatically correct sentences)

The essay will probably evolve in the next couple of years as the College Board receives feedback from graders, test-takers, and college admissions officers. The best preparation for this moving target is to pay attention to the material you read in school or for pleasure and to *hone* (sharpen) your own essay-writing skills as you do your homework and school exams.

Are you energetic enough to try an essay? Here's a sample question, along with some points you might make in your answer. (Don't peak until you've finished drafting your own answer, though!)

As you read the passage, consider how Keith Sawyer uses the following:

- Evidence such as facts or examples to support his ideas

- Logic to develop the argument and link claims and supporting evidence

- Style choices — appeals to emotion, figurative language, word choice, and so forth — to add to the persuasive power of the argument

The following passage is taken from Zig Zag: The Surprising Path to Great Creativity, *by Keith Sawyer (Wiley).*

Most successful creativity comes through the process you begin without knowing what the real problem is. The parameters aren't clearly specified, the goal isn't clear, and you don't even know what it would look like if you did solve the problem. It's not obvious how to apply your past experience solving other problems. And there are likely to be many different ways to approach a solution.

These grope-in-the-dark situations are the times you need creativity the most. And that's why successful creativity always starts with asking.

It's easy to see how business innovation is propelled by formulating the right question, staying open to new cues, and focusing on the right problem. But it turns out the same is true of world-class scientific creativity. "The formulation of a problem is often more essential than its solution," Albert Einstein declared. "To raise new questions, new possibilities, to regard old problems from a new angle, requires creative imagination and marks real advances in science." Einstein went on to say, "For the detective the crime is given," he concluded. "The scientist must commit his own crime as well as carry out the investigation."

If the right "crime" — the right puzzle or question — is crucial for business and scientific breakthroughs, what about breakthroughs in art or poetry or music? A great painting doesn't emerge from posing a good question — does it?

The pioneering creativity researcher Mihaly Csikszentmihalyi of the University of Chicago decided to answer that question. He and a team of fellow psychologists from the University of Chicago spent a year at the School of the Art Institute of Chicago, one of the top art schools in the United States. "How do creative works come into being?" they wanted to know. They set up an "experimental studio" in which they positioned two tables. One was empty, the other laden with a variety of objects, including a bunch of grapes, a steel gearshift, a velvet hat, a brass horn, an antique book, and a glass prism. They then recruited thirty-one student artists and instructed them to choose several items, position them any way they liked on the empty table, and draw the arrangement.

After observing the artists, Csikszentmihalyi was able to identify two distinct artistic approaches. One group took only a few minutes to select and pose the objects. They spent another couple of minutes sketching an overall composition and the rest of their time refining, shading, and adding details to the composition. Their approach was to formulate a visual problem quickly and then invest their effort in solving that problem.

The second group could not have been more different. These artists spent five or ten minutes examining the objects, turning them around to view them from all angles. After they made their choices, they often changed their minds, went back to the table, and replaced one object with another. They drew the arrangement for twenty or thirty minutes and then changed their minds again, rearranged the objects, and erased and completely redrew their sketch. After up to an hour like this, the students in this group settled on an idea and finished the drawing in five or ten minutes. Unlike the first group — which spent most of the time *solving* a visual problem — this group was *searching* for a visual problem. The research team called this a "problem-finding" creative style.

Which artists' work was more creative: that of the problem solvers or that of the problem finders? Csikszentmihalyi asked a team of five Art Institute professors to rate the creativity of each drawing. With few exceptions, the problem finders' drawings were judged far more creative than the problem solvers' — even though their exploratory process left them much less time to devote to the final image, which was all the judges (who knew nothing of the process involved) were evaluating.

The most creative artists were those who focused on asking the right question.

Six years after the students graduated, the most successful of the students had become well known in the art world, with work in leading New York galleries and even in the permanent collections of famous museums. And these successful artists were by and large the problem finders back when they were in art school. They were the artists who focused on asking the right question.

Write an essay in which you explain how Sawyer constructs an argument to persuade the reader that creativity comes from asking the right question. In your essay, discuss how Sawyer uses one or more of the elements of style listed above, or other elements, to strengthen the logic and persuasiveness of his argument. Focus on the most important features of the passage. Do not explain whether you agree or disagree with Sawyer's ideas. Instead, concentrate on how he builds a persuasive case.

Many paths lead to a good answer to this essay question. Here are some possible ideas you may mention in your essay:

- **Appeal to ethos:** The essay quotes Albert Einstein, a widely known genius who came up with startling new ideas about the nature of space and time.

- **Appeal to logos:** The experiment is factual, explaining how the artists worked and how their creations were evaluated. The use of a factual example is classic *logos*.

- **The essay structure moves logically from point to point:** Right in the first paragraph, Sawyer explains the problem — which is that you often don't know what the problem actually is. Next Sawyer moves to Einstein's views on creativity and finally to the art experiment, both of which confirm that the most creative people fiddle around with the question before they seek the answer.

- **The crucial point appears as a single sentence that itself is a single paragraph:** "The most creative artists were those who focused on asking the right question." To add emphasis, Sawyer places that line in italics.

- **Sawyer's diction is simple and straightforward:** Few words are above elementary-school level, though the concepts Sawyer discusses are fairly sophisticated. He speaks directly to readers with the second-person pronoun *you*. The result is a recommendation that any reader can understand and adopt.

- **References to more than one field:** By mentioning "business innovation," Einstein, and art, Sawyer underlines the universality of his view of creativity.

You probably came up with additional ideas. As long as they relate to the passage, you're in good shape. To structure your answer essay, you may begin by stating Sawyer's views on creativity in greater detail. An analysis of *logos* and *ethos* could be grouped in one paragraph. A discussion of Sawyer's structure, including the single-sentence paragraph, form another logical group. Finally, examples of simple diction and second-person point of view create a third paragraph. The "universality" analysis in the last bullet point could be included in this paragraph because that approach is still another attempt to connect with the reader.

Refreshing the Math

The topics in the new SAT Mathematics section are remarkably similar to the old SAT math section, with brain-teaser questions on number properties, exponents, solving for *x*, coordinate geometry, three-dimensional shapes, and word problems. The new SAT Math section brings trigonometry to the table but only in a limited form.

The arrangement of the new SAT Math section is different from the organization of the old SAT math. Rather than force-feeding you three math sections that are pretty much the same, the new SAT force-feeds you two math sections that are different.

- ✔ **Calculator section:** You work 37 questions in 55 minutes, and, yes, you get to use your calculator.

  - Thirty of these questions have multiple-choice answers, but unlike the old SAT with five answers to choose from, the new SAT has four answers to choose from. See? It's already easier. These questions are worth one point each.

  - Six of these questions have grid-in answers, where you find a numeric answer and then bubble in the actual numbers in a grid. The old SAT had this type of grid-in, too. These questions are also worth one point each.

  - One math question is an Extended Thinking question, which is just like the other math questions only with a few more layers of complication. This question also has a grid-in answer, but unlike the other questions, this one is worth four points.

- ✔ **No-calculator section:** You work 20 questions in 25 minutes, and, you guessed it, you can't use a calculator. These questions are more concept-based than arithmetic-based but are no less challenging.

  - Fifteen of these questions have multiple-choice answers, with four answers to choose from, and are worth one point each.

  - Five of these questions have grid-in answers and are also worth one point each.

Unlike the old SAT, the new SAT doesn't take away points for a wrong multiple-choice answer. (This is called a "penalty for guessing.") If you have no idea how to answer a question, flip a mental coin and bubble in an answer. However, if you're prepared for the test, this won't really happen.

Spread across these two math sections are four primary categories of math questions.

- ✔ **Algebra:** The SAT calls this category "Heart of Algebra." These questions ask you to analyze and solve equations, create expressions to represent quantity relationships, and rearrange and interpret formulas.

- ✔ **Problem solving and data analysis:** These questions examine whether you can analyze relationships by using ratios and proportions as well as interpret and summarize graphs.

- ✔ **Geometry:** The SAT calls this category "Additional Topics in Math," but the description reads like basic geometry: lines and angles, flat shapes, three-dimensional shapes, and trigonometry.

- ✔ **Advanced math:** The SAT calls this "Passport to Advanced Math." Questions here ask you to solve quadratic equations and rewrite expressions based on the math structure. It's also a useful bucket for questions that don't fall into the other three categories.

In the following sections, you find a sample question from each category. These questions and solutions specifically demonstrate how to approach the questions using logic and sense.

Algebra

Algebra problems deal with finding the value of x where x can change or have more than one possible value. The key is remembering that x represents a number, so you can plug a number in for x to get a sense of how the problem works.

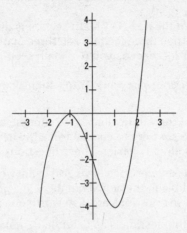

The preceding graph represents $f(x)$. How many solutions does the equation $f(x) = -1$ have?

(A) zero

(B) one

(C) two

(D) three

The correct answer is Choice (D). Like most SAT math questions, this question takes a simple, basic concept and presents it in a way that you're not used to. It's almost like a different language. On the xy-plane, $f(x)$ is exactly the same as y. You can literally cross off "$f(x)$" and write in "y." If $f(x) = -1$, it simply means that $y = -1$. Draw a line where $y = -1$, and you see that it crosses the graph of $f(x)$ three times. In SAT-speak, this means that $f(x) = -1$ has three solutions.

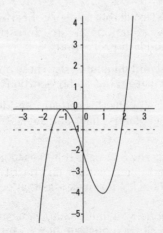

Problem solving and data analysis

Problem solving and data analysis problems challenge your ability to make sense of a mass of text or data. Don't get lost in all the information; skim through it for the pieces that you need, usually numbers. When there's a graph, skip the graph and go straight to the question. This example question refers to the following chart, which represents the money that Sita had in her bank accounts during the years 2008, 2009, and 2010.

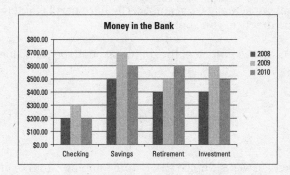

If Sita's money in her retirement account in 2008 represents 0.1% of the bank's money, how much money is in the bank?

(A) $400

(B) $4,000

(C) $40,000

(D) $400,000

The correct answer is Choice (D). The SAT likes to present simple, basic math in a seemingly complicated context. Never mind all the data in the graph; you need exactly one single unit of data from the graph, which is the 2008 value of Sita's retirement account: $400. If this is 0.1% of the bank's money, you can set up a proportion with x as the total money in the bank. Cross-multiply to get $400,000 = 0.1x$, and $x = \$400,000$.

Geometry

Geometry problems are based on the properties of the shapes. For example, two crossing lines create identical opposite angles, the angles of a triangle total 180°, and each point on a given circle is the exact same distance (*radius*) from the center. Pay attention to these properties when solving these problems.

If a pizza with a 12-inch diameter is cut into 8 equal slices, what is the area of 1 slice?

(A) 2.25π

(B) 4.5π

(C) 9π

(D) 18π

The correct answer is Choice (B). The SAT asks questions that seem to be challenging, but there's always a neat, simple way to solve the problem. Never mind that only on the SAT would a pizza have a diameter. At 12 inches across, the pizza has a radius (again, only on the SAT) of 6 inches. The area of a circle is $\pi \cdot r^2$, so the area of the pizza is 36π. If the pizza is cut into 8 equal slices, then each slice has an area of $\frac{36\pi}{8}$, *or* 4.5π. On your next date, if you have pizza, try not to show off this knowledge.

Advanced math

Advanced math problems have hidden tricks and patterns that make the problem seemingly challenging but actually very simple. The hard part is finding the underlying pattern, but with a little practice, you spot these easily.

If $x^2 + 2xa + a^2 = 16$, which of the following could be the value of $x + a?$

(A) –8

(B) –4

(C) –2

(D) 2

The correct answer is Choice (B). Before jumping into the math, look for some way to simplify the expression. It may take a moment to spot the trick, but in this problem, it's that $x^2 + 2xa + a^2$ can be factored into $(x + a)^2$. By now, you're learning to expect such *chicanery* (trickery) from the SAT. Rewrite the equation as $(x + a)^2 = 16$. If you take the square root of both sides, you get $x + a$ equals 4 or –4. The question asks which *could* be the right answer, and only –4 is a possible answer.

As *artful* (crafty) as the SAT may be, the questions are always fair. A question such as this never has both 4 and –4 as answer choices, unless it also has other information, such as $x + a < 0$, to clarify which answer is true.

These sample questions are true to form of almost all SAT math questions. The SAT is *sly* (also crafty), but with practice and guidance for what to look for, you'll be more so. Even if at first you struggle with the practice test questions in Chapter 6, the important thing is that you look back on them and grasp exactly what the trick is, so you always have the key to solving the problem. The answers and explanations in Chapter 7 highlight these tricks. Soon you'll spot them on your own and can *bequeath* (pass on) this book to younger students. Better yet, sell it to them.

Part II

The Moment of Truth: Taking a Practice Test

Duplicating the Test Environment

You can take this SAT practice test little by little — a section at a time, perhaps. You get the most out of mimicking real test conditions, though, by following these guidelines:

- ✔ **Set aside an entire morning for the test.** Turn off your phone, computer, siblings, and pets. (How do you turn off a dog or a brother? Barricade your room and send them outside!)

- ✔ **Use the answer sheet and bubble your answers with a #2 pencil,** just as you would on the real SAT. If you choose to write the essay, have a couple of sheets of lined paper ready. Write with a pencil, unless you're sure that a computer-based testing center is nearby and available to you. (Not many exist right now.)

- ✔ **Watch the clock, or better yet, set a timer.** Don't go over time on any section, and don't return to a section once you've started a new one.

- ✔ **Don't turn to a new section before the official time is up.** If you finish early, recheck your work or just relax in your chair.

- ✔ **Take breaks.** Take one ten-minute break after the Writing and Language section. If you're writing the essay, take another ten-minute break before you start that task.

For Dummies can help you get ready for the SAT. Check out www.dummies.com for more information!

In this part ...

✔ Find out how prepared you are for the SAT by taking full-length practice test sections.

✔ Score your test quickly with the answer key.

✔ Discover how to improve your performance by perusing the answer explanations for all the practice questions.

Chapter 4

Section I: Reading

· ·

*I*n the Reading section of the SAT, you have 65 minutes to read four single passages and one pair of passages. You answer 52 questions based on what is stated or implied in the passages and the accompanying graphs, charts, diagrams, or other visual elements. Single passages range from 500 to 750 words; the total number of words in the paired passage set is also 500 to 750 words.

The answers and explanations for the questions in this practice test are in Chapter 7. Go through the explanations to all the questions, even if you answered the question correctly. The explanations are a good review of the reading-comprehension techniques you need for the SAT and also may help you improve your vocabulary skills.

Answer Sheet for Section 1, Reading

1. Ⓐ Ⓑ Ⓒ Ⓓ
2. Ⓐ Ⓑ Ⓒ Ⓓ
3. Ⓐ Ⓑ Ⓒ Ⓓ
4. Ⓐ Ⓑ Ⓒ Ⓓ
5. Ⓐ Ⓑ Ⓒ Ⓓ
6. Ⓐ Ⓑ Ⓒ Ⓓ
7. Ⓐ Ⓑ Ⓒ Ⓓ
8. Ⓐ Ⓑ Ⓒ Ⓓ
9. Ⓐ Ⓑ Ⓒ Ⓓ
10. Ⓐ Ⓑ Ⓒ Ⓓ
11. Ⓐ Ⓑ Ⓒ Ⓓ

12. Ⓐ Ⓑ Ⓒ Ⓓ
13. Ⓐ Ⓑ Ⓒ Ⓓ
14. Ⓐ Ⓑ Ⓒ Ⓓ
15. Ⓐ Ⓑ Ⓒ Ⓓ
16. Ⓐ Ⓑ Ⓒ Ⓓ
17. Ⓐ Ⓑ Ⓒ Ⓓ
18. Ⓐ Ⓑ Ⓒ Ⓓ
19. Ⓐ Ⓑ Ⓒ Ⓓ
20. Ⓐ Ⓑ Ⓒ Ⓓ
21. Ⓐ Ⓑ Ⓒ Ⓓ
22. Ⓐ Ⓑ Ⓒ Ⓓ

23. Ⓐ Ⓑ Ⓒ Ⓓ
24. Ⓐ Ⓑ Ⓒ Ⓓ
25. Ⓐ Ⓑ Ⓒ Ⓓ
26. Ⓐ Ⓑ Ⓒ Ⓓ
27. Ⓐ Ⓑ Ⓒ Ⓓ
28. Ⓐ Ⓑ Ⓒ Ⓓ
29. Ⓐ Ⓑ Ⓒ Ⓓ
30. Ⓐ Ⓑ Ⓒ Ⓓ
31. Ⓐ Ⓑ Ⓒ Ⓓ
32. Ⓐ Ⓑ Ⓒ Ⓓ
33. Ⓐ Ⓑ Ⓒ Ⓓ

34. Ⓐ Ⓑ Ⓒ Ⓓ
35. Ⓐ Ⓑ Ⓒ Ⓓ
36. Ⓐ Ⓑ Ⓒ Ⓓ
37. Ⓐ Ⓑ Ⓒ Ⓓ
38. Ⓐ Ⓑ Ⓒ Ⓓ
39. Ⓐ Ⓑ Ⓒ Ⓓ
40. Ⓐ Ⓑ Ⓒ Ⓓ
41. Ⓐ Ⓑ Ⓒ Ⓓ
42. Ⓐ Ⓑ Ⓒ Ⓓ
43. Ⓐ Ⓑ Ⓒ Ⓓ
44. Ⓐ Ⓑ Ⓒ Ⓓ

45. Ⓐ Ⓑ Ⓒ Ⓓ
46. Ⓐ Ⓑ Ⓒ Ⓓ
47. Ⓐ Ⓑ Ⓒ Ⓓ
48. Ⓐ Ⓑ Ⓒ Ⓓ
49. Ⓐ Ⓑ Ⓒ Ⓓ
50. Ⓐ Ⓑ Ⓒ Ⓓ
51. Ⓐ Ⓑ Ⓒ Ⓓ
52. Ⓐ Ⓑ Ⓒ Ⓓ

Reading

Time: 65 minutes for 52 questions

Directions: Read these passages and answer the questions that follow based on what is stated or implied in the passages and accompanying diagrams, charts, or graphs.

Questions 1–10 refer to the following excerpt from O Pioneers, *by Willa Cather.*

Line The Bergson homestead was easier to find than many another, because it overlooked a shallow, muddy stream. This creek gave a sort of identity to the farms that bordered upon it. Of all the bewildering things about a new country, the absence of human landmarks is one of the most depressing and disheartening. The houses were small and were usually

(05) tucked away in low places; you did not see them until you came directly upon them. Most of them were built of the sod itself, and were only the inescapable ground in another form. The roads were but faint tracks in the grass, and the fields were scarcely noticeable. The record of the plow was insignificant, like the feeble scratches on stone left by prehistoric races, so indeterminate that they may, after all, be only the markings of glaciers, and not a record of

(10) human strivings.

In eleven long years John Bergson had made but little impression upon the wild land he had come to tame. It was still a wild thing that had its ugly moods; and no one knew when they were likely to come, or why. Mischance hung over it. Its Genius was unfriendly to man. The sick man was feeling this as he lay looking out of the window, after the doctor had left him,

(15) on the day following his daughter Alexandra's trip to town. There it lay outside his door, the same land, the same lead-colored miles. He knew every ridge and draw and gully between him and the horizon. To the south, his plowed fields; to the east, the sod stables, the cattle corral, the pond — and then the grass.

Bergson went over in his mind the things that had held him back. One winter his cattle had

(20) perished in a blizzard. The next summer one of his plow horses broke its leg in a prairie dog hole and had to be shot. Another summer he lost his hogs from disease, and a valuable stallion died from a rattlesnake bite. Time and again his crops had failed. He had lost two children, boys, that came between Lou and Emil, and there had been the cost of sickness and death. Now, when he had at last struggled out of debt, he was going to die himself.

(25) He was only forty-six, and had, of course, counted on more time.

Bergson had spent his first five years getting into debt, and the last six getting out. He had paid off his mortgages and had ended pretty much where he began, with the land. He owned exactly six hundred and forty acres of what stretched outside his door; his own original homestead and timber claim, making three hundred and twenty acres, and the half-section

(30) adjoining, the homestead of a younger brother who had given up the fight, gone back to Chicago to work in a fancy bakery and distinguish himself in a Swedish athletic club. So far John had not attempted to cultivate the second half-section, but used it for pasture land, and one of his sons rode herd there in open weather.

John Bergson had the Old-World belief that land, in itself, is desirable. But this land was an

(35) enigma. It was like a horse that no one knows how to break to the harness, that runs wild and kicks things to pieces. He had an idea that no one understood how to farm it properly, and this he often discussed with Alexandra. Their neighbors, certainly, knew even less about farming than he did. Many of them had never worked on a farm until they took up their homesteads. They had been handworkers at home; tailors, locksmiths, joiners, cigar-

(40) makers, etc. Bergson himself had worked in a shipyard.

Go on to next page

1. Which of the following statements best describes John Bergson's attitude toward nature?

   (A) Natural features are beautiful.

   (B) Human beings should not interfere with nature.

   (C) Nature is inferior to human construction.

   (D) Wilderness areas are preferable to cities and towns.

2. Which lines provide the best evidence for the answer to Question 1?

   (A) Lines 2–4 ("Of all . . . disheartening.")

   (B) Lines 11–12 ("In eleven . . . tame.")

   (C) Lines 13–15 ("The sick man . . . town.")

   (D) Lines 34–35 ("But this land . . . enigma.")

3. What best fits the definition of "human strivings" in the context of Line 10?

   (A) "shallow, muddy stream" (Line 2)

   (B) "bewildering things" (Line 3)

   (C) "new country" (Line 3)

   (D) "faint tracks in the grass" (Line 7)

4. The comparison between the plowed fields and "the feeble scratches on stone left by prehistoric races" (Line 8) serves to

   (A) introduce the idea of human weakness

   (B) show that this settlement has a long history

   (C) emphasize the primitive quality of the farming

   (D) describe the effects of glaciers

5. The "Genius" mentioned in Line 13 may best be defined as

   (A) intelligence

   (B) spirit

   (C) brain

   (D) type

6. Which of the following best explains the meaning of the pronoun "this" in Line 14?

   (A) the amount of work Bergson had invested in his land

   (B) the symptoms of Bergson's illness

   (C) Bergson's bad mood

   (D) the wild nature of Bergson's land

7. The list of events in the third paragraph (Lines 19–25) serve to

   (A) illustrate Bergson's bad luck

   (B) show that Bergson was unprepared for farming

   (C) emphasize some hope for the future of Bergson's farm

   (D) provide information about Bergson's character

8. In the context of Line 35, the land is "an enigma" because

   (A) it differs from the land of the Old World

   (B) the settlers don't know how to farm it

   (C) it is too dry

   (D) John Bergson planned poorly

9. John Bergson would most likely agree with which statement?

   (A) No matter how prepared you are, you will not survive on the frontier.

   (B) Life in the Old World is superior to life on the frontier.

   (C) Survival on the frontier is dependent upon animals.

   (D) Life on the frontier is not always easy.

10. Which lines are the best evidence supporting the answer to Question 9?

    (A) Lines 4–5 ("The houses were small . . . them.")

    (B) Lines 11–12 ("In eleven long . . . tame.")

    (C) Lines 19–24 ("One winter . . . sickness and death.")

    (D) Lines 36–38 ("He had an idea . . . than he did.")

Go on to next page

Questions 11–20 refer to the following passage and diagram from A Brief History of the Olympics, by David C. Young (Wiley).

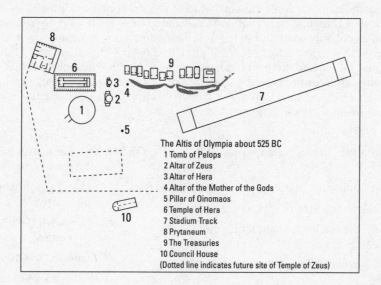

The Altis of Olympia about 525 BC
1 Tomb of Pelops
2 Altar of Zeus
3 Altar of Hera
4 Altar of the Mother of the Gods
5 Pillar of Oinomaos
6 Temple of Hera
7 Stadium Track
8 Prytaneum
9 The Treasuries
10 Council House
(Dotted line indicates future site of Temple of Zeus)

Line "Victory by speed of foot is honored above all." Those are the words of Xenophanes, a sixth century BCE philosopher who objected to athletes and their popularity. The phrase "speed of foot" may recall the words expressed in Homer's *Odyssey* stressing the glory which an athlete may win "with his hands or with his feet." The shortest foot race, the *stade*, was one

(05) length of the stadium track, the practical equivalent of our 200 meter dash (actually, only 192.27 meters at Olympia, the site of the original Olympic games). Greek tradition held that this 200 meter race was the first and only event held at the first Olympiad in 776 BCE.

The name of the winner of the 200 appears first in all lists of victors in any Olympiad. Some people think that the *stade* winner had the year named after him. This is not really true.

(10) Most Greek states had other means of dating any given year, usually by the name of one or more political leaders. But when Hippias of Elis compiled his catalogue of victors, the *stade* victor obviously headed his list for each individual Olympiad. Perhaps because the Olympic festival was one of the few truly international institutions in Greece, later Greeks found it convenient to use the sequence of Olympiads as a chronological reference. Thus an entry in

(15) Julius Africanus' text will read, for example, "Olympiad 77, Dandis of Argos [won] the stade." Subsequent years within the Olympiad are simply viewed as Olympiad 77, years two, three, and four.

As one would expect, methods of running seem to be no different then from now. Several vase paintings show a group of runners rather close to one another, their bodies pitched

(20) forward, their arms making large swings up and down. These are clearly runners in the 200, for modern sprinters look much the same. So also distance runners can be easily identified. Like their modern counterparts, they can run upright, with less arc in their leg movements, and their arms dangle comfortably at their sides. Some of these ancient athletes developed the effective strategy of hanging back with the rest of the pack, reserving some strength

(25) until near the end. Then they would suddenly break away from the rest and close with a strong spurt of speed, as if barely tired, passing the leaders who became weak and faded. Ancient sources never specify the exact number of laps in the distance race, and modern opinions vary greatly. The most widely accepted number is 20 laps, a distance of a little over 3845 meters (2.36 miles), more than double our classic distance race of 1500 meters.

Go on to next page

(30) The ancient stadium was shaped very differently from the modern one. It was almost twice as long as ours, and about half as wide. There was no course around an infield, no infield at all, just adjacent lanes for the runners. The athletes had therefore no gradual turns around a curve at each end, as in a modern stadium. Stephen Miller, excavator at Nemea, found a posthole not far from the north end of the stadium. He conjectures that it held a turning

(35) post. It is highly likely that, in the distance race, such a single turning post for all athletes was probably used. But in the 400, down and back, the runner would need to turn sharply around the post. Most scholars think that each 400 runner would have had his own turning post. Otherwise there would have been too much congestion at that only turn. A few vases show athletes not patently sprinters or distance runners going around a turning post. In

(40) one, a judge stands watch. But if each 400 meter runner had his own turning post, the scene probably shows a distance race.

11. The quotations in this passage primarily serve to

    (A) offer conflicting opinions

    (B) establish an authoritative voice

    (C) invite the reader to conduct further research

    (D) give a sense of Greek literary style

12. According to information presented in the passage and accompanying figure, the area where the Olympiad took place

    (A) devoted less space to athletic contests than to other activities

    (B) was consecrated to the gods

    (C) was rectangular in shape

    (D) fulfilled athletes' needs

13. In the context of Line 5, what is the best definition of "practical"?

    (A) hands-on

    (B) likely to succeed

    (C) realistic

    (D) pragmatic

14. According to the passage, which of the following statements is correct?

    (A) Winners earned glory for the state they represented, not for themselves.

    (B) The Greek stadium was similar to modern arenas.

    (C) The Olympiads served as a common reference point for time.

    (D) Running styles differed in ancient times.

15. Which lines provide supporting evidence for the answer to Question 14?

    (A) Line 2 ("philosopher who objected . . . popularity")

    (B) Lines 4–5 ("one length of the stadium . . . games")

    (C) Line 18 ("As one would expect . . . now")

    (D) Lines 13–14 ("later Greeks . . . reference")

16. The author's comment "as one would expect" (Line 18) is probably based on

    (A) his own experience as a runner

    (B) the fact that human anatomy does not change

    (C) recent archeological discoveries

    (D) information from contemporary literature

17. In the context of Line 28, what is the best definition of "accepted"?

    (A) generally believed

    (B) taken from what is offered

    (C) approved

    (D) admitted

18. With which statement would the author of this passage most likely agree?

    (A) History is an accurate record of events.

    (B) The best historical evidence comes from literature.

    (C) Historians should tap many sources of information.

    (D) Unless written records exist, history must remain unknown.

Go on to next page

19. Which lines support the answer to Question 18?

    (A) Lines 27–28 ("Ancient sources . . . vary greatly.") and Lines 37–38 ("Most scholars think . . . post.")

    (B) Line 1 ("Victory by speed . . . above all.") and Lines 3–4 ("words expressed . . . with his feet.")

    (C) Lines 11–12 ("Hippias of Elis . . . Olympiad") and Lines 15–16 ("Julius Africanus . . . stade")

    (D) Line 8 ("The name of the winner . . . Olympiad.") and Lines 19–20 ("vase paintings . . . up and down.")

20. The discussion of turning posts in Lines 38–41 ("A few vases show . . . distance race.")

    (A) illustrates the difference between modern and ancient Olympic events

    (B) shows how historians misinterpret evidence

    (C) reveals a question that can be solved only by more research

    (D) explains the limits of ancient athletes

Questions 21–31 refer to the following passages. Passage I is an excerpt from Novel Plant Bioresources, *by Gurib Fakim (Wiley). Passage II is an excerpt from* Biology For Dummies, *2nd Edition, by Rene Kratz and Donna Siegfried (also published by Wiley).*

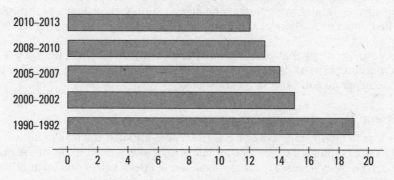

Percentage of Undernourished Persons in the World, 1990–2013

United Nations Food and Agricultural Organization

Passage I

Line The world still faces tremendous challenges in securing adequate food that is healthy, safe, and of high nutritional quality for all and doing so in an environmentally sustainable manner. With the growing demand of an expected 9 billion people by 2050, it remains unclear how our current global food system will cope. Currently, 868 million people suffer from hunger,

(05) while micronutrient deficiencies, known as hidden hunger, undermine the development, health, and productivity of over 2 billion people. The estimation of plant species that exist in the world is between 250,000 and 400,000. As many as 80% of the world's people depend on traditional medicines, which involve the use of plant extracts or their active principles for their primary health care needs. Plant diversity has a critical role to play in addressing the

(10) food and nutrition security and medicinal needs of the people of this world. Plant diversity is

Go on to next page ➡

not evenly distributed across the world and tends to be concentrated in specific, diversity-rich areas. It is generally known that most diversity of species occurs within the warm regions of the tropics and less diversity exists in temperate regions of the world.

(15) Plants are an intricate part of all our ecosystems. Besides the obvious provisioning of food in ensuring that people are food and nutritionally secured, many plants contribute directly to our agriculture by providing valuable traits and genes used by modern-day breeders for crop improvement, in particular those plants which are closely related to crop plants, the so-called "crop wild relatives," and restore health in an important human adaptation, as fundamental a feature of human culture as is use of fire, tools, and speech. Having evolved

(20) over millennia, the knowledge, cultural traditions, and medicinal resources of many human societies may be rapidly disappearing with the loss of cultural and biological diversity.

In spite of this great diversity of plants on Earth and the fundamental role they play, the story of crops and humanity has shown an increasing reliance on a small proportion of plant species used by humans. The beginnings of exploitation of plant diversity for food and

(25) nutrition are as old as humankind, and early hunter gatherers in pre-agricultural times would have exploited their local environment for readily available fruits, berries, seeds, flowers, shoots, storage organs, and fleshy roots to complement meat obtained from hunting.

Furthermore, crop plants have resulted in an even greater reliance by humans on much

(30) reduced plant diversity than was previously used for food by pre-agricultural human societies. More than 70,000 plants are known to have edible parts. The world's food comes from about 100 plant species, based on calories, protein, and fat supply. However, only four crop species (maize, wheat, rice, and sugar) supply almost 60% of the calories and protein in the human diet. There are thousands of plant species with neglected potential utility.

(35) Many studies show that plant diversity is globally threatened. Recently a group of international experts called for the development of a global program for the conservation of useful plants and associated knowledge.

Passage II

The loss in biodiversity could have effects beyond just the loss of individual species. Living

(40) things are connected to each other and their environment in how they obtain food and other resources necessary for survival. If one species depends on another for food, for example, then the loss of a prey species can cause a decline in the predator species.

Some species, called keystone species, are so connected with other organisms in their environment that their extinction changes the entire composition of species in the area.

(45) As biodiversity decreases, keystone species may die out, causing a ripple effect that leads to the loss of many more species. If biodiversity gets too low, then the future of life itself becomes threatened. An example of a keystone species is the purple seastar, which lives on the northwest Pacific coast of the United States. Purple seastars prey on mussels in the intertidal zone. When the seastars are present, they keep the mussel population in check,

(50) allowing a great diversity of other marine animals to live in the intertidal zone. If the seastars are removed from the intertidal zone, however, the mussels take over, and many species of marine animals disappear from the environment.

Biodiversity increases the chance that at least some living things will survive in the face of large changes in the environment, which is why protecting it is crucial. The combined effect

(55) of various human actions in Earth's ecosystems is reducing the planet's biodiversity. In fact, the rate of extinctions is increasing along with the size of the human population. No one knows for certain how extensive the loss of species due to human impacts will ultimately be, but there's no question that human practices such as hunting and farming have already caused numerous species to become extinct.

Go on to next page

21. In the context of Line 3, what is the best definition of "demand"?

    (A) command

    (B) insistence

    (C) popularity

    (D) need

22. Taken as a whole, these passages may best be characterized as

    (A) an argument in favor of biodiversity

    (B) a comparison of current and prehistoric food supplies

    (C) a description of how ecosystems work

    (D) an inventory of popular crops and endangered species

23. Of the four lines listed here, which represents the best evidence for the answer to Question 22?

    (A) Lines 3–4 ("With the growing . . . cope.") and Lines 41–42 ("If one species depends . . . predator species.")

    (B) Lines 6–7 ("The estimation . . . 400,000.") and Line 47 ("An example . . . purple seastar.")

    (C) Lines 19–21 ("Having evolved . . . diversity.") and Lines 48–49 ("Purple seastars . . . intertidal zone.")

    (D) Lines 46–47 ("If biodiversity . . . threatened") and Lines 53–54 ("Biodiversity increases the chance . . . environment.")

24. With which statement would the authors of both passages most likely agree?

    (A) Human beings should not exploit plant and animal resources.

    (B) Slowing the rate of extinctions is no longer possible.

    (C) Reliance on a small number of food sources causes problems.

    (D) Keystone species should be protected at all costs.

25. The "9 billion people" mentioned in Line 3

    (A) rely on our current food system

    (B) are those experiencing hunger when the passage was written

    (C) represent the estimated population of Earth in 2050

    (D) is the most likely number of undernourished people in 2050

26. In the context of Line 11, which of the following best expresses the meaning of "concentrated"?

    (A) distributed

    (B) thought about

    (C) given attention

    (D) grouped

27. Passage II implies that large populations of mussels

    (A) become keystone species in their environment

    (B) displace other species

    (C) do not compete for food with purple seastars

    (D) are a major cause of extinctions

28. According to the passages and accompanying graph, which of these statements is true?

    I.   The percentage of the population with an adequate amount of food rose from 1990 to 2013.

    II. The number of people who lack important nutrients is greater than the number of people who are considered "undernourished" in official surveys.

    III. The number of animal species providing food for human beings is decreasing.

    (A) I only

    (B) II only

    (C) I and II

    (D) II and III

29. The author of Passage I presents statistics about the types of crops humans cultivate for food in order to

    (A) illustrate overreliance on a small number of species

    (B) explain why food resources are scarce

    (C) show that food is harvested inefficiently

    (D) reveal the shortcomings of the average person's diet

Go on to next page ⟶

30. Which of the following would the author of Passage II most likely support?

    (A) a drive to clean seashore areas

    (B) a petition to ban the cultivation of mussels

    (C) a program to preserve keystone species in forested areas

    (D) a required course in marine biology

31. In comparison with Passage I, Passage II is

    (A) more focused on food supplies

    (B) less concerned with plant diversity

    (C) more focused on plants

    (D) more focused on ecosystems

Questions 32–42 refer to the following passage from President Abraham Lincoln's Second Inaugural Address, the speech he gave in 1865 when he took the oath of office for his second term as President. The Civil War between the North and the South was nearing its end as Lincoln spoke.

Line Fellow Countrymen:

At this second appearing to take the oath of the presidential office, there is less occasion for an extended address than there was at the first. Then a statement, somewhat in detail, of a course to be pursued, seemed fitting and proper. Now, at the expiration
(05) of four years, during which public declarations have been constantly called forth on every point and phase of the great contest which still absorbs the attention, and engrosses the energies of the nation, little that is new could be presented. The progress of our arms, upon which all else chiefly depends, is as well known to the public as to myself; and it is, I trust, reasonably satisfactory and encouraging to all. With high
(10) hope for the future, no prediction in regard to it is ventured.

On the occasion corresponding to this four years ago, all thoughts were anxiously directed to an impending civil-war. All dreaded it — all sought to avert it. While the inaugural address was being delivered from this place, devoted altogether to saving the Union without war, insurgent agents were in the city seeking to destroy it without
(15) war — seeking to dissolve the Union, and divide effects, by negotiation. Both parties deprecated war; but one of them would make war rather than let the nation survive; and the other would accept war rather than let it perish. And the war came.

One eighth of the whole population were colored slaves, not distributed generally over the Union, but localized in the Southern part of it. These slaves constituted a
(20) peculiar and powerful interest. All knew that this interest was, somehow, the cause of the war. To strengthen, perpetuate, and extend this interest was the object for which the insurgents would rend the Union, even by war; while the government claimed no right to do more than to restrict the territorial enlargement of it.

Neither party expected for the war, the magnitude, or the duration, which it has
(25) already attained. Neither anticipated that the cause of the conflict might cease with, or even before, the conflict itself should cease. Each looked for an easier triumph, and a result less fundamental and astounding. Both read the same Bible, and pray to the same God; and each invokes His aid against the other. It may seem strange that any men should dare to ask a just God's assistance in wringing their bread from the sweat
(30) of other men's faces; but let us judge not that we be not judged. The prayers of both could not be answered; that of neither has been answered fully.

The Almighty has His own purposes. "Woe unto the world because of offences! for it must needs be that offences come; but woe to that man by whom the offence cometh!"

Go on to next page

(35) If we shall suppose that American Slavery is one of those offences which, in the providence of God, must needs come, but which, having continued through His appointed time, He now wills to remove, and that He gives to both North and South, this terrible war, as the woe due to those by whom the offence came, shall we discern therein any departure from those divine attributes which the believers in a Living God always ascribe to Him? Fondly do we hope — fervently do we pray — that this mighty scourge of war may speedily pass away.

(40) Yet, if God wills that it continue, until all the wealth piled by the bond-man's two hundred and fifty years of unrequited toil shall be sunk, and until every drop of blood drawn with the lash, shall be paid by another drawn with the sword, as was said three thousand years ago, so still it must be said "the judgments of the Lord, are true and righteous altogether."

(45) With malice toward none; with charity for all; with firmness in the right, as God gives us to see the right, let us strive on to finish the work we are in; to bind up the nation's wounds; to care for him who shall have borne the battle, and for his widow, and his orphan — to do all which may achieve and cherish a just, and a lasting peace, among ourselves, and with all nations.

32. In the context of Line 4, what is the best definition of "course"?

(A) study

(B) plan

(C) field

(D) lessons

33. In paragraph one (Lines 1–10), what does Lincoln imply about the war?

(A) Too much has been said about the war.

(B) Politicians have paid too little attention to it.

(C) His side is winning.

(D) No one will be satisfied with the result.

34. Which of the following is the best evidence supporting the answer to the previous question?

(A) Lines 2–3 ("less occasion . . . first")

(B) Line 4 ("course . . . proper")

(C) Lines 6–7 ("absorbs . . . presented")

(D) Line 9 ("reasonably . . . all")

35. Lincoln most likely states that "little that is new could be presented" (Line 7) because

(A) the war monopolizes the attention and resources of the nation

(B) he has no vision of a peaceful future

(C) the public's views are unknown

(D) his listeners are not ready for the future

36. According to Lincoln, during his first inauguration

(A) citizens generally agreed on a plan for his administration

(B) the movement to disband the nation had already begun

(C) there was unconditional support for war

(D) negotiations to avoid war had already ended

37. In the context of Line 20, what is the best definition of "interest"?

(A) attention

(B) issue

(C) benefit

(D) problem

38. In the fourth paragraph of Lincoln's speech (Lines 24–31) he

(A) pleads for an end to war

(B) emphasizes what both sides have in common

(C) dismisses the concerns of his opponents

(D) argues that the war was unavoidable

39. What is the best evidence for the answer to Question 38?

(A) Lines 24–25 ("the magnitude . . . attained")

(B) Line 26 ("the conflict itself . . . cease")

(C) Lines 27–28 ("Both read . . . same God")

(D) Line 31 ("neither has . . . fully")

Go on to next page

40. Throughout the speech, Lincoln uses the pronouns *we*, *us* and *our* to refer to

    (A) Northerners

    (B) Southerners

    (C) those present during the speech

    (D) both Northerners and Southerners

41. Lincoln's purpose in giving this speech was most likely to

    (A) proclaim victory

    (B) condemn slavery

    (C) emphasize the idea of a united country

    (D) encourage his troops

42. The dominant strategy in this speech is

    (A) an appeal to logic

    (B) a reliance on religious principles

    (C) an appeal for personal support

    (D) a condemnation of opponents

Questions 43–52 refer to the following information, excerpted and adapted from The Story of Eclipses, *by George F. Chambers (London: George Newnes, Ltd.).*

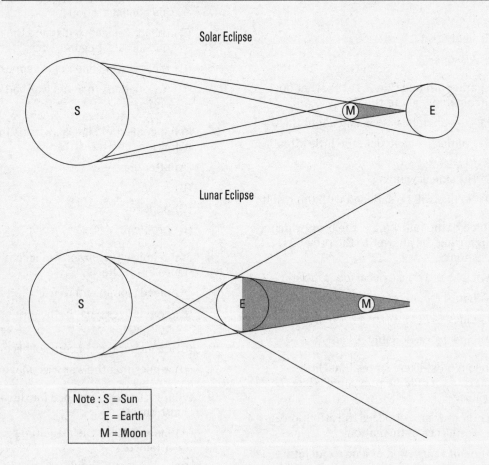

Solar Eclipse

Lunar Eclipse

Note : S = Sun
E = Earth
M = Moon

Go on to next page

Line   The primary meaning of the word "eclipse" is a disappearance, the covering over of
something by something else. This apparently crude definition will be found, on
investigation, to represent precisely the facts of the case.

(05)   As the Earth and the Moon are solid bodies, each must cast a shadow into space as the
result of being illuminated by the Sun, a source of light. The various bodies which together
make up the Solar System, the planets and their moons, are constantly in motion.
Consequently, if we imagine a line to be drawn between any two bodies at any given time,
such a line will point in a different direction at another time, and so it may occasionally
happen that three of these ever-moving bodies will sometimes come into one and the same
(10)   straight line. When one of the extremes of the series of three bodies in a common direction
is the Sun, the intermediate body deprives the other extreme body, either wholly or partially, of illumination. When one of the extremes is the Earth, the intermediate body inter-
cepts, wholly or partially, the other extreme body from the view of observers situated at
places on the Earth which are in the common line of direction, and the intermediate body is
(15)   seen to pass over the other extreme body as it enters upon or leaves the common line of
direction. The phenomena resulting from such contingencies of position and direction
are variously called *eclipses*, *transits*, and *occcultations*, according to the relative apparent
magnitudes of the interposing and obscured bodies, and according to the circumstances
that attend them.

(20)   The Earth moves round the Sun once in every year; the Moon moves round the Earth once
in every lunar month (27 days). The Earth moves round the Sun in a certain plane, an imaginary surface on which a line drawn between any two points lies flat. If the Moon as the
Earth's companion moved round the Earth in the same plane, an eclipse of the Sun would
happen regularly every month when the Moon was in "conjunction," the "New Moon,"
(25)   during which the Moon is not visible in the sky, and also every month at the intermediate
period there would be a total eclipse of the Moon on the occasion of every "opposition," or
"Full Moon," when the Moon appears as a complete circle. But because the Moon's orbit
does not lie in quite the same plane as the Earth's, but is inclined at an angle averaging
about $5\frac{1}{8}°$, the actual facts are different. Instead of there being in every year about 25
(30)   eclipses (of the sun and of the moon in nearly equal numbers), which there would be if the
orbits had identical planes, there are only a very few eclipses in the year. Never, under the
most favorable circumstances, are there more than seven, and sometimes as few as two.

Eclipses of the Sun are more numerous than those of the Moon in the proportion of about
three to two, yet at any given place on the Earth more lunar eclipses are visible than solar
(35)   eclipses, because eclipses of the Moon, when they occur, are visible over the whole hemisphere, or half, of the Earth that is turned towards the Moon. The area over which a total
eclipse of the Sun is visible is just a belt of the Earth no more than about 150 to 170 miles
wide.

43. In the context of Line 1, the best meaning of
"primary" is

(A) earliest

(B) most primitive

(C) most direct

(D) most basic

44. According to the explanation in this
passage, which of the following could be
considered "an eclipse"?

(A) mixing cream into a cup of coffee

(B) an apple sitting in front of a grape

(C) two stars shining brightly in the sky

(D) Mars and Venus

Go on to next page

45. What is the best evidence for the answer to Question 44?

    (A) Lines 1–2 ("disappearance . . . else")

    (B) Lines 5–6 ("various bodies . . . motion")

    (C) Lines 16–19 ("The phenomena resulting . . . attend them.")

    (D) Lines 27–29 ("the Moon's orbit . . . different")

46. The most common stylistic devices in this passage are

    (A) definition and example

    (B) narration and characterization

    (C) description and figurative language

    (D) analogies and implied comparison

47. In the context of Line 11, what is the best definition of "extreme"?

    (A) exaggerated

    (B) highest degree

    (C) outer

    (D) most advanced

48. Why does any line "drawn between any two bodies at any given time" (Line 7) "point in a different direction at another time" (Line 8)?

    (A) The line is not real.

    (B) The paths of the Sun, Moon, and Earth are unknown.

    (C) The Moon and Earth are in constant motion.

    (D) The Earth is larger than the Moon.

49. Which of the following supports the answer to Question 48?

    (A) Lines 4–5 ("each must cast . . . source of light")

    (B) Lines 8–10 ("occasionally happen . . . the same straight line")

    (C) Lines 20–21 ("The Earth moves . . . 27 days.")

    (D) Lines 35–36 ("when they occur . . . towards the Moon")

50. According to the diagram, if a person stands on the unilluminated portion of the Earth during a lunar eclipse, what does he see?

    (A) a portion of the Moon

    (B) the Moon's shadow

    (C) the Sun's shadow

    (D) the Earth's shadow

51. Information about the Moon's orbit being "inclined at an angle averaging about 5⅛°" (Lines 28–29) relative to the Earth

    (A) illustrates the unimportance of the Moon

    (B) emphasizes that eclipses of the Sun are more widely seen than eclipses of the Moon

    (C) explains why the Earth, Moon, and Sun do not align more frequently

    (D) shows that eclipses of the Sun and Moon occur in equal numbers

52. According to the passage, which statement is true?

    (A) The Sun casts shadows on the Moon and on the Earth.

    (B) More people see eclipses of the Moon than eclipses of the Sun.

    (C) Our Solar System includes the Sun, stars, planets, and moons.

    (D) Eclipses of the Sun cover a larger area than eclipses of the Moon.

STOP DO NOT TURN THE PAGE UNTIL TOLD TO DO SO. DO NOT RETURN TO A PREVIOUS TEST.

Chapter 5

Section II: Writing and Language

• •

*T*he Writing and Language section of the SAT is divided into two parts: one multiple-choice section, which is required, and one optional essay.

For the multiple-choice section, you have 35 minutes to read four passages, each accompanied by 11 questions. The essay, which is always the last section of the test, eats up 50 minutes of your morning. It's based on one passage that is 650 to 750 words long.

The answers and explanations for the questions in this practice test are in Chapter 7. Go through the explanations to all the questions, even if you answered the question correctly. The explanations are a good review of the grammar and writing techniques you need for the SAT and also may include tricks, shortcuts, and strategies to help you on exam day.

Answer Sheet for Section 2, Writing and Language

1. Ⓐ Ⓑ Ⓒ Ⓓ
2. Ⓐ Ⓑ Ⓒ Ⓓ
3. Ⓐ Ⓑ Ⓒ Ⓓ
4. Ⓐ Ⓑ Ⓒ Ⓓ
5. Ⓐ Ⓑ Ⓒ Ⓓ
6. Ⓐ Ⓑ Ⓒ Ⓓ
7. Ⓐ Ⓑ Ⓒ Ⓓ
8. Ⓐ Ⓑ Ⓒ Ⓓ
9. Ⓐ Ⓑ Ⓒ Ⓓ

10. Ⓐ Ⓑ Ⓒ Ⓓ
11. Ⓐ Ⓑ Ⓒ Ⓓ
12. Ⓐ Ⓑ Ⓒ Ⓓ
13. Ⓐ Ⓑ Ⓒ Ⓓ
14. Ⓐ Ⓑ Ⓒ Ⓓ
15. Ⓐ Ⓑ Ⓒ Ⓓ
16. Ⓐ Ⓑ Ⓒ Ⓓ
17. Ⓐ Ⓑ Ⓒ Ⓓ
18. Ⓐ Ⓑ Ⓒ Ⓓ

19. Ⓐ Ⓑ Ⓒ Ⓓ
20. Ⓐ Ⓑ Ⓒ Ⓓ
21. Ⓐ Ⓑ Ⓒ Ⓓ
22. Ⓐ Ⓑ Ⓒ Ⓓ
23. Ⓐ Ⓑ Ⓒ Ⓓ
24. Ⓐ Ⓑ Ⓒ Ⓓ
25. Ⓐ Ⓑ Ⓒ Ⓓ
26. Ⓐ Ⓑ Ⓒ Ⓓ
27. Ⓐ Ⓑ Ⓒ Ⓓ

28. Ⓐ Ⓑ Ⓒ Ⓓ
29. Ⓐ Ⓑ Ⓒ Ⓓ
30. Ⓐ Ⓑ Ⓒ Ⓓ
31. Ⓐ Ⓑ Ⓒ Ⓓ
32. Ⓐ Ⓑ Ⓒ Ⓓ
33. Ⓐ Ⓑ Ⓒ Ⓓ
34. Ⓐ Ⓑ Ⓒ Ⓓ
35. Ⓐ Ⓑ Ⓒ Ⓓ
36. Ⓐ Ⓑ Ⓒ Ⓓ

37. Ⓐ Ⓑ Ⓒ Ⓓ
38. Ⓐ Ⓑ Ⓒ Ⓓ
39. Ⓐ Ⓑ Ⓒ Ⓓ
40. Ⓐ Ⓑ Ⓒ Ⓓ
41. Ⓐ Ⓑ Ⓒ Ⓓ
42. Ⓐ Ⓑ Ⓒ Ⓓ
43. Ⓐ Ⓑ Ⓒ Ⓓ
44. Ⓐ Ⓑ Ⓒ Ⓓ

Writing and Language

Time: 35 minutes for 44 questions

Directions: Choose the best answer based on what you see in the passage and diagrams, charts, or graphs.

Passage 1

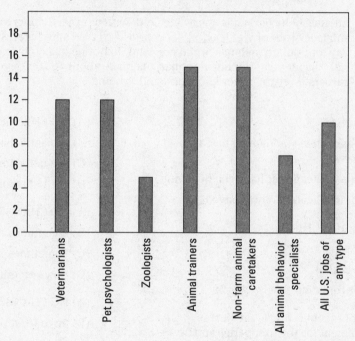

Projected Job Growth : Animal Care and Service Workers

Source : U.S. Bureau of Labor Statistics

Illustration by John Wiley & Sons, Inc.

Dr. Vint Virga stares at Molly, a [1] <u>Barbary sheep. Molly has been behaving</u> strangely since her tail was amputated after an accident. Molly spends almost all of her time nervously checking for flies that she used to bat away easily with her tail. Dr. Virga decides that Molly has a phobia, an irrational fear. He prescribes medication and works to ease her fears by distracting her with food and [2] <u>subtracting</u> her anxiety level so that she can stand quietly when insects do approach. Virga travels from zoo to zoo, where he solves the problems of animals like Molly. [3]

Animal behaviorists may be veterinarians, as Dr. Virga is, or animal trainers, zoologists, college professors, zookeepers, and many other types of workers who specialize in animals. Animal behaviorists interpret how individuals or whole populations of animals eat, move, rest, play, and [4] <u>relating to their environment</u>. Identifying problems, [5] <u>the animals may be treated by the behaviorist</u> with medicine or behavior modification techniques.

The field is new. In earlier times, what was going on inside an animal's mind was not a concern. The Greek philosopher Aristotle (384 to 322 BCE) said that animals couldn't think.

Go on to next page ▶

French philosopher Rene Descartes (1596 to 1650 CE) compared the cry of an animal to the squeak of a clock spring, a mechanical reaction. Even in the modern era, behaviorists are [6] now sometimes accused of anthropomorphism, ascribing human traits to nonhuman beings. The danger of this approach is that animals won't be seen for who they are and their behavior may be misinterpreted. Scientist Philip Low says, "If you ask my colleagues whether animals have emotions and thoughts, many will drop their voices or change the subject."

Almost [7] anyone, who has pets, sees evidence of animals' inner life. Recent studies show that elephants recognize themselves [8] when they see themselves in a mirror, and many species, such as fruit flies, ants, and chimpanzees cooperate. Zookeepers frequently report that animals grieve when others housed in the same enclosure die. In 2012, a number of scientists in Cambridge University signed a declaration asserting that animals probably have emotions and consciousness, [9] but they are self-aware.

Animals behaviorism is a growing field, with a projected increase in jobs in its various subspecialties of [10] at least 11%, according to the United States Bureau of Labor Statistics. Pay for nonfarm animal caretakers, who do not need a college degree, averages around $20,000 per year, though veterinarians make about $85,000 a year. In general, higher paid careers [11] return better education and training.

1. (A) NO CHANGE
   (B) Barbary sheep, and Molly has been behaving
   (C) Barbary sheep that has been behaving
   (D) Barbary sheep. Molly behaved

2. (A) NO CHANGE
   (B) lowering
   (C) increasing
   (D) subordinating

3. Which of the following is the best improvement for the first paragraph?
   (A) Add this sentence to the end of the paragraph: "He is an animal behaviorist."
   (B) Delete this sentence: "Dr. Virga decides that Molly has a phobia, an irrational fear."
   (C) Add this sentence to the beginning of the paragraph: "Barbary sheep are also known as aoudads."
   (D) Delete "since her tail was amputated after an accident."

4. (A) NO CHANGE
   (B) environmental relation of animals
   (C) the way in which they relate to their environment
   (D) relate to their environment

5. (A) NO CHANGE
   (B) the animals, treat by the behaviorist,
   (C) the behaviorist treats the animals
   (D) the behaviorists, they treat the animals

6. (A) NO CHANGE
   (B) sometimes are now accused
   (C) sometimes accused
   (D) now sometimes accusing

7. (A) NO CHANGE
   (B) anyone who has pets sees
   (C) anyone, who has pets, see
   (D) anyone who have pets see

8. (A) NO CHANGE
   (B) when one sees itself
   (C) seeing itself
   (D) when it sees itself

9. (A) NO CHANGE
   (B) being self-aware
   (C) though they are self-aware
   (D) and they are self-aware

Go on to next page

10. (A) NO CHANGE
    (B) about 7%
    (C) perhaps 11%
    (D) 15% less

11. (A) NO CHANGE
    (B) mirror
    (C) result
    (D) reflect

Passage II

Trenches in World War I

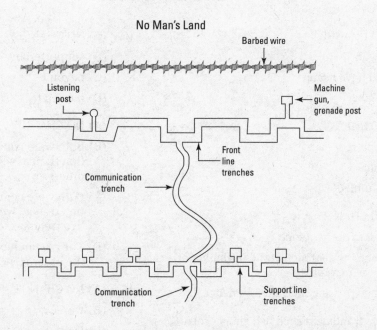

About a century ago, in August, 1914, what participants called "The Great War" and, ironically, "The War to End All Wars," [12] had begun. We know this conflict as World War I, one of the bloodiest periods in human history. When it ended in 1918, about 9 million soldiers were dead and the health of 7 million more was permanently [13] disabled. They were never again healthy enough to return to their former way of life.

[1] About 25,000 miles of trenches — enough to circle the globe at the Equator — were dug to protect and shelter soldiers from enemy fire. [2] Trenches on both sides — the Allies and their foes, the Central Powers — were only a few hundred yards apart. [14] [3] A unique feature of World War I was the trench system. [4] A typical trench, diagrammed in the Figure 1, were about 6 to 8 feet deep and topped on the enemy side by sandbags.

[15] The frontline trench had short protrusions designed for shooting machine guns or launching grenades. Listening to the enemy was also done there. The frontline trenches were [16] backed by support trenches a few hundred yards away, where medical officers tended the wounded and where other, non-combat activities took place. [17] Both were connected by a communication trench, which was parallel to the others. Because fire could spread quickly in a straight line, the trenches, [18] laid out in a zigzag pattern, with fire breaks every few yards.

[1] The trenches were not pleasant places. [19] [2] Sandbags, thin iron sheets, or sticks supported the walls. [3] The frontline trench was protected by a line of barbed wire, and the area in between was called "No Man's Land" because to be caught there was to risk instant

Go on to next page

death. [4] Soldiers were stationed in the frontline trenches for 3 to 7 days and then rotated to support trenches for [20] <u>they're</u> rest period, eventually returning to the front line. [5] Despite four years of war and huge numbers of deaths, neither side succeeded in moving its trenches more than a short distance into enemy territory. [21] [6] <u>The soldiers spent the day in a mixture of boredom and terror. [7] They felt boredom waiting for an attack and terror when one occurred</u>.

[1] Few civilians understood the conditions the soldiers faced. [2] A sample trench in a London park appeared comfortable. [3] Soldiers who had seen the real trenches were often bitter when they saw the luxury of the sample trench, which did not resemble those on the front. [22]

12. (A) NO CHANGE
     (B) began
     (C) will have begun
     (D) begun

13. (A) NO CHANGE
     (B) impaired
     (C) unfit
     (D) wounded

14. (A) NO CHANGE
     (B) Delete the sentence.
     (C) Place the sentence at the beginning of the paragraph.
     (D) Place the sentence after Sentence 4.

15. (A) The frontline trench had short protrusions designed for shooting machine guns or launching grenades, listening to the enemy was also done there.
     (B) Listening to the enemy, the frontline trench had short protrusions designed for shooting machine guns or launching grenades.
     (C) The frontline trench had short protrusions designed for shooting machine guns or launching grenades, and they could listen to the enemy there.
     (D) The frontline trench had short protrusions designed for shooting machine guns, launching grenades, and listening to the enemy.

16. (A) NO CHANGE
     (B) supported by
     (C) beyond
     (D) backed to

17. (A) NO CHANGE
     (B) Both were connected by a communication trench, which cut across the others.
     (C) Both were connected by a communication trench, which was near the other two trenches.
     (D) The communication trench connected the other trenches by being parallel.

18. (A) NO CHANGE
     (B) were laid
     (C) lain
     (D) were lying

19. What should be added, if anything, after Sentence 1 in paragraph four?
     (A) NO CHANGE
     (B) There were many trenches, and many soldiers.
     (C) Fire was a danger.
     (D) Wooden floor boards covered a drainage area, but the narrow trenches were never quite dry.

Go on to next page

20. (A) NO CHANGE
    (B) there
    (C) their
    (D) soldier's

21. (A) The soldiers spent the day in a mixture of boredom, waiting for an attack, and terror, when one occurred.
    (B) Bored and terrified, the soldiers spent the day.
    (C) The soldiers spent the day in a mixture of boredom and terror, feeling boredom waiting for an attack and terror when one occurred.
    (D) The soldiers spent the day in a mixture of boredom and terror, boredom waiting for an attack and terror in an attack.

22. What would be the best change, if any, to the last paragraph?
    (A) NO CHANGE
    (B) Add this sentence before Sentence 2: "Soldiers saw that the trench in the park was different."
    (C) Add this sentence after Sentence 3: "It was all too easy for civilians to see this conflict as "The Great War," but the war was not always great in the eyes of those who fought it."
    (D) Add this sentence after Sentence 3: "The war ended in 1918."

Passage III

Ten years old, hair in pigtails, [23] sitting in the back seat of our pink-and-white car, which is on the way to Vermont. The elderly next door neighbors in our quiet suburb, the Hamiltons, have been pressing my parents about a vacation rental near their house on the shore of Lake Saint Catherine, and [24] they've finally given in. Mommy and Daddy don't like the Hamiltons, restricting contact with the couple to one dinner when we first [25] moved in, which Alfred Hammond served food for each of us at the head of the table. When our family ate dinner, platters circled the table, unless they were in reach of long arms and serving spoons. In that case everyone simply grabbed what [26] they wanted and ate it.

[27] [1] We greet the Hamiltons. [2] The two-room cabin is made of fragrant wood (pine, I think), and the air is blessedly cool. [3] (Even at that age I couldn't take heat.) [4] Jimmy and I sleep in the bedroom in bunks attached to the wall near our parents' air mattress.

[28] [1] The water of Lake Saint Catherine is pretty deep. [2] There's no beach, just a dock, but we can both swim, so Jimmy and I jump off the dock, paddle around until we reach the little wooden ladder and then climb up to start all over again. [3] My father works in an office, and he has only three weeks' vacation time each year. [4] Once or twice Daddy rows across the lake in a little wooden boat, but he clearly doesn't [29] dote on the effort. [5] We also fish from the dock. [6] I remember holding a dead, wriggling, two-inch something that I throw back in the water as soon as Daddy takes a picture of it.

On some days we go sightseeing. I remember a marble quarry at Barre. Mostly (typical of my mother's priorities) we stay in the gift shop, where [30] shards of marble are on sale, as well as some finished items. In my view the big slabs look like tombstones, [31] and the tombstones make me nervous and they make me glad when we leave.

[32] [1]We take another trip, at night, to a drive-in movie. [2] All I remember of that evening is a white-knuckle trip back to the cabin. [3] I can tell from my parents' voices that they're scared, too. [4] At each junction they confer rapidly, and we do find the cottage, but I spend the time worrying that we'll drive off the road and into a ditch, or worse, [33] that we'll just keep driving forever.

Go on to next page ⟶

23. (A) NO CHANGE
    (B) sitting, I
    (C) I'm sitting
    (D) having sat

24. (A) NO CHANGE
    (B) the Hamiltons have
    (C) my parents have
    (D) they have

25. (A) NO CHANGE
    (B) moved in which
    (C) moved,
    (D) moved in, at which

26. (A) NO CHANGE
    (B) he or she wanted and ate
    (C) they wanted,
        and ate
    (D) was wanting and eating

27. (A) NO CHANGE
    (B) We greeted the Hamiltons.
    (C) In Vermont, we greet the Hamiltons.
    (D) Greeting the Hamiltons

28. What change, if any, should be made to the third paragraph?
    (A) NO CHANGE
    (B) Delete Sentence 1.
    (C) Delete Sentence 3.
    (D) Change Sentence 5 to "We also fish from the dock, which is made of wood."

29. (A) NO CHANGE
    (B) be fond of
    (C) evaluate
    (D) relish

30. (A) NO CHANGE
    (B) columns
    (C) vestiges
    (D) rubbles

31. (A) NO CHANGE
    (B) which make me nervous and glad to
    (C) and the tombstones make me nervous and glad when we
    (D) nervous and glad when we

32. Which of the following would improve the last paragraph?
    (A) Before Sentence 1, add: "We take many trips throughout my childhood."
    (B) Delete Sentence 1.
    (C) Add after Sentence 2: "Without street lights, the country roads appear dark and dangerous to me, a city girl."
    (D) Add after Sentence 4: "I enjoyed the movie, though."

33. (A) NO CHANGE
    (B) that will just drive forever
    (C) just driving forever
    (D) that we'll just drive forever

Go on to next page

Passage IV

In 1859, [34] Thomas Austin an Australian who enjoyed hunting, released 24 rabbits on his land. The hunter stated that "introduction of a few rabbits could do little harm" and "might provide a touch of home." [35] He liked to hunt. Before this time, [36] there was some domestic rabbits in Australia, mostly in cages or other enclosures. With a moderate climate, the wild rabbits bred all year round. [37] Soon Australia had a rabbit problem. More than 200 million rabbits were living there. Farms and wooded areas were overrun with rabbits; millions of dollars worth of crops were destroyed, and many young trees died when the rabbits chewed rings around the bark. [38] Less trees led to increased erosion and loss of topsoil. The hunter never thought that 24 rabbits would become a national problem. His action is an example of human [39] intervention in a natural ecosystem that is too complicated to understand completely.

[40] [1] The same kind of action has been taking place in Arizona. [2] Water is precious in Arizona's desert environment. [3] Tamarisk trees, a non-native species that was imported about a century ago and planted to fight soil erosion, have very deep roots. [4] They soak up a lot of water — up to 200 gallons a day for a mature tree. [5] Chopping down tamarisks or burning them didn't solve the problem, as the trees quickly grew back. [6] So tamarisk beetles, small insects about a centimeter long, were [41] initiated into the environment.

The number of tamarisk trees [42] have decreased because of the beetles. The policy seems to be a success. However, not all factors are known. What about the birds that live in tamarisk trees? Will they die as their habitat changes? When the tamarisk trees are gone, will the beetles attack other trees? If too many trees disappear, will the soil erode, harming the habitat of still more organisms?

No one knows the answer to these questions, because nature is too complex for limited human intelligence to understand completely. [43] One answer that is known to humans is that interfering with the environment cannot be stopped, and some unforeseen consequences will occur. It is what human beings do when they plant crops, construct cities, dam rivers, and tap into energy and water supplies. The human effect on nature is everywhere.

[44] [1] The solution is not to stay away from nature, but instead to be more careful in how we interact with nature. [2] Studying how organisms interact is important. [3] You should also check consumption. [4] Scientists must provide information on the environment and the potential consequences of changes to the environment. [5] Citizens must tailor their behavior according to that information.

---

34. (A) NO CHANGE
    (B) Thomas Austin an Australian, that enjoyed hunting, released
    (C) an Australian who enjoyed hunting and was named Thomas Austin released
    (D) Thomas Austin, an Australian who enjoyed hunting, released

35. (A) NO CHANGE
    (B) Delete the underlined words.
    (C) Thomas Austin liked to hunt.
    (D) Thomas Austin, he liked to hunt.

36. (A) NO CHANGE
    (B) their was
    (C) there were
    (D) their were

Go on to next page ⟶

37. (A) Soon Australia had a rabbit problem, but more than 200 million rabbits were living there.
    (B) More than 200 million rabbits were living there soon, and Australia had a rabbit problem.
    (C) More than 200 million rabbits soon lived in Australia, and they caused a problem.
    (D) Soon, with more than 200 million rabbits, Australia had a problem.

38. (A) NO CHANGE
    (B) Fewer trees led
    (C) Less trees lead
    (D) Fewer trees lead

39. (A) NO CHANGE
    (B) intercession
    (C) interruption
    (D) affectation

40. Which of the following changes, if any, should be made to paragraph two?
    (A) NO CHANGE
    (B) Add this sentence after Sentence 5: "The trees wither and die when the beetles feed on them."
    (C) Delete Sentence 4.
    (D) Delete Sentence 5.

41. (A) NO CHANGE
    (B) started
    (C) commenced
    (D) introduced

42. (A) NO CHANGE
    (B) have been decreasing
    (C) has decreased
    (D) decreasing

43. (A) NO CHANGE
    (B) What we do know
    (C) One answer known to humans
    (D) Known

44. Which of the following would be the best change to the last paragraph?
    (A) Add this sentence before Sentence 1: "Everything changes."
    (B) Add this sentence after Sentence 2: "Interacting with nature should always be considered before acting."
    (C) Delete Sentence 3 and insert this sentence instead: "Monitoring consumption of water, energy, and other resources is also crucial."
    (D) Add this sentence at the end of the paragraph: "Nature is our most important resource."

STOP   DO NOT TURN THE PAGE UNTIL TOLD TO DO SO.
DO NOT RETURN TO A PREVIOUS TEST.

The Essay

> **Time:** 50 minutes
>
> As you read this passage, consider how the author uses the following:
>
> • Facts, examples, and other types of evidence to support his assertions
>
> • Logical structure to link ideas and evidence
>
> • Elements of style, such as appeals to reason, word choice, and so forth, to make his case

The following is excerpted from The NOW Habit at Work, *by Neil Fiore (Wiley).*

In *Emotions Revealed: Recognizing Faces and Feelings to Improve Communication and Emotional Life,* Paul Ekman describes how to determine if people are lying by observing the universal microfacial expressions of anger, disgust, fear, joy, sadness, surprise, and contempt. Even if a person doesn't consciously know that you're lying or trying to cover up your true feelings, she will have a gut reaction that something isn't right. The hidden and often subconscious message embedded in your words, actions, facial expressions, and body movements reflects your true attitude and affects your energy level. Others may subconsciously notice the disconnection between your words and your nonverbal message and sense that you're not telling the whole truth.

We all know how leaders often preach one thing and do the opposite, causing their actions to contradict their words and professed beliefs. Colleagues have said of Viktor Frankl, a Holocaust survivor and founder of logotherapy [a form of psychotherapy], that when he advocated that every life has meaning, there was a unity between his words, his actions, and the way he lived.

Are your messages and actions integrated around your higher brain and executive self? You may want to examine how your actions and stated values are aligned with what you consciously and rationally believe. Then ask yourself, "Is my walk congruent with my talk? What underlying and overarching beliefs are revealed in the way I talk to myself and others? Is it all struggle and sacrifice?" Are you saying, "Life is tough and then you die" or "You have to work harder, but it will never be good enough"?

Even more powerful than your actual words is the impact of what you think and expect from yourself and others. Research has repeatedly shown that teachers who are led to believe that certain children have high intelligence scores paid more attention to those children and encouraged them to do their best. As a result, the test scores and behaviors of those children improved significantly, even though these children actually had the lowest intelligence scores in their class. The teachers' beliefs and expectations influenced their behavior and had real, positive effects on the children they taught. The same is true of your beliefs about yourself and your employees.

Beliefs and expectations influence much more than just your attitude. What you believe affects your brain and body the way a placebo pill — an inert substance presented as effective medicine — improves depression and physical symptoms in as many as 30% of patients. You might want to consider, therefore, telling yourself, your children, and your employees that you believe in them and their willingness to learn and do good work and that you are a firm supporter of their worth and truer, higher self. You may find it more effective to communicate to yourself and others that life is an interesting puzzle, a mystery that you were meant to solve and that you have the innate ability to do so. Your words and actions

Go on to next page

might communicate that you enjoy your life and are optimistic about your future. Pessimists tend to be more accurate about the odds of success but give up sooner, while optimists keep trying until they come up with a creative solution and are happier. You may want to communicate the message "You're going to make it, even though you don't know how. Something will come to you, and you will pick yourself up and stand on your own two feet."

Being optimistic is one way to motivate yourself to keep taking another shot at success and face the inevitable challenges of life while hoping to turn lemons into lemonade. An optimistic view of life — and of yourself, your co-workers, and employees — will turn your mind toward what's going well and has the effect of lowering depression. Research by Martin Seligman of the University of Pennsylvania's Positive Psychology Center found that those who wrote down three things that went well each day and their causes every night for one week had a significant increase in happiness and a decrease in depressive symptoms. Remarkably, the participants got so much value out of the exercise that they continued on their own for more than six months, and when tested again, they were found to be even happier. Other research points to the importance of meaning in life — interest in exploring a sense of purpose or mission for one's life — as contributing to happiness, healthy self-esteem, and effectiveness.

Directions: Write an essay in which you analyze how Fiore makes an argument that one's true beliefs influence both self and others. In your essay, discuss how Fiore uses the elements of style listed before the passage, as well as other stylistic choices, to strengthen his argument. Focus your response on the most important aspects of the passage.

Do not explain whether you agree or disagree with Fiore. Instead, focus on how the author builds his argument.

Go on to next page

Go on to next page

Go on to next page

STOP DO NOT TURN THE PAGE UNTIL TOLD TO DO SO.
DO NOT RETURN TO A PREVIOUS TEST.

Chapter 6

Section III: Math

· ·

The Math section of the SAT consists of a series of questions intended to measure general mathematics skills and problem-solving ability. The questions are based on short readings that may include a graph, chart, or figure.

The Math section is divided into two subsections. For the first section, you may use a calculator, and you have 55 minutes to complete the section. For the second section, you may not use a calculator, and you have only 25 minutes to complete the section.

The answers and explanations for the questions in this practice test are in Chapter 7. Go through the explanations to all the questions, even if you answered the question correctly. The explanations are a good review of the mathematical techniques discussed in the book and also may include tricks, shortcuts, and strategies to help you on exam day.

Formulas you may need are given on the first page of each math section, before the first question. Only some of the questions require you to use a formula, and you may not need all the formulas given.

Note: Most of these formulas are basic concepts that you should know, such as the area of a triangle and the circumference of a circle. However, they serve as a good reference in case you draw a blank on the question.

Answer Sheet for Section 3, Math

Calculator Section

1. Ⓐ Ⓑ Ⓒ Ⓓ
2. Ⓐ Ⓑ Ⓒ Ⓓ
3. Ⓐ Ⓑ Ⓒ Ⓓ
4. Ⓐ Ⓑ Ⓒ Ⓓ
5. Ⓐ Ⓑ Ⓒ Ⓓ
6. Ⓐ Ⓑ Ⓒ Ⓓ

7. Ⓐ Ⓑ Ⓒ Ⓓ
8. Ⓐ Ⓑ Ⓒ Ⓓ
9. Ⓐ Ⓑ Ⓒ Ⓓ
10. Ⓐ Ⓑ Ⓒ Ⓓ
11. Ⓐ Ⓑ Ⓒ Ⓓ
12. Ⓐ Ⓑ Ⓒ Ⓓ

13. Ⓐ Ⓑ Ⓒ Ⓓ
14. Ⓐ Ⓑ Ⓒ Ⓓ
15. Ⓐ Ⓑ Ⓒ Ⓓ
16. Ⓐ Ⓑ Ⓒ Ⓓ
17. Ⓐ Ⓑ Ⓒ Ⓓ
18. Ⓐ Ⓑ Ⓒ Ⓓ

19. Ⓐ Ⓑ Ⓒ Ⓓ
20. Ⓐ Ⓑ Ⓒ Ⓓ
21. Ⓐ Ⓑ Ⓒ Ⓓ
22. Ⓐ Ⓑ Ⓒ Ⓓ
23. Ⓐ Ⓑ Ⓒ Ⓓ
24. Ⓐ Ⓑ Ⓒ Ⓓ

25. Ⓐ Ⓑ Ⓒ Ⓓ
26. Ⓐ Ⓑ Ⓒ Ⓓ
27. Ⓐ Ⓑ Ⓒ Ⓓ
28. Ⓐ Ⓑ Ⓒ Ⓓ
29. Ⓐ Ⓑ Ⓒ Ⓓ
30. Ⓐ Ⓑ Ⓒ Ⓓ

31.
32.
33.
34.
35.
36.
37.

No-Calculator Section

1. Ⓐ Ⓑ Ⓒ Ⓓ   4. Ⓐ Ⓑ Ⓒ Ⓓ   7. Ⓐ Ⓑ Ⓒ Ⓓ   10. Ⓐ Ⓑ Ⓒ Ⓓ   13. Ⓐ Ⓑ Ⓒ Ⓓ

2. Ⓐ Ⓑ Ⓒ Ⓓ   5. Ⓐ Ⓑ Ⓒ Ⓓ   8. Ⓐ Ⓑ Ⓒ Ⓓ   11. Ⓐ Ⓑ Ⓒ Ⓓ   14. Ⓐ Ⓑ Ⓒ Ⓓ

3. Ⓐ Ⓑ Ⓒ Ⓓ   6. Ⓐ Ⓑ Ⓒ Ⓓ   9. Ⓐ Ⓑ Ⓒ Ⓓ   12. Ⓐ Ⓑ Ⓒ Ⓓ   15. Ⓐ Ⓑ Ⓒ Ⓓ

16.   17.   18.   19.   20.

Math

Calculator Section

Time: 55 minutes for 37 questions

Directions: This section contains two different types of questions. For Questions 1–30, choose the best answer to each question and darken the corresponding oval on the answer sheet. For Questions 31–37, follow the separate directions provided before those questions.

Notes:

✔ You may use a calculator.

✔ All numbers used in this exam are real numbers.

✔ All figures lie in a plane.

✔ All figures may be assumed to be to scale unless the problem specifically indicates otherwise.

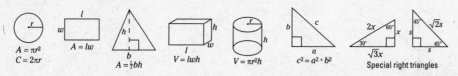

1. A box has exactly 11 marbles in it. Three of the marbles are green, six are yellow, and the rest are red. If one marble is drawn at random from the box, what is the probability that the marble is red?

   (A) $\frac{1}{11}$

   (B) $\frac{1}{9}$

   (C) $\frac{2}{11}$

   (D) $\frac{2}{9}$

2. Three cars drove past a speed-limit sign on a highway. Car A was traveling twice as fast as Car B, and Car C was traveling 20 miles per hour faster than Car B. If Car C was traveling at 60 miles per hour, how fast was Car A going?

   (A) 20 miles per hour

   (B) 30 miles per hour

   (C) 40 miles per hour

   (D) 80 miles per hour

Go on to next page

3. No two points on the graph have the same *y*-coordinate. Which of the following graphs has this property?

(A)

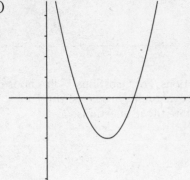

(B)

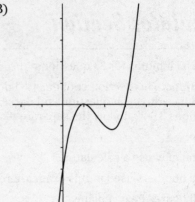

(C)

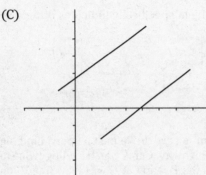

(D)

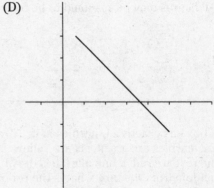

4. For integers *a*, *b*, and *c*, let $a \# b \# c$ be defined by $a \# b \# c = a^2 - bc + b$. What is the value of $6 \# 3 \# 4$?

(A) 3

(B) 12

(C) 27

(D) 30

5. If 3 less than twice a number is 13, what is 5 times the number?

(A) 8

(B) 30

(C) 40

(D) 50

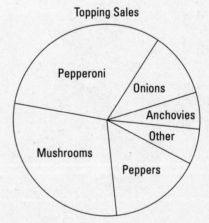

6. According to the circle graph, how many of the pizza toppings individually represent more than 25 percent of total sales?

(A) one

(B) two

(C) three

(D) four

Go on to next page

7. If $\left|10 - 3y\right| < 3$, which of the following is a possible value of y?

   (A) 0

   (B) 1

   (C) 2

   (D) 3

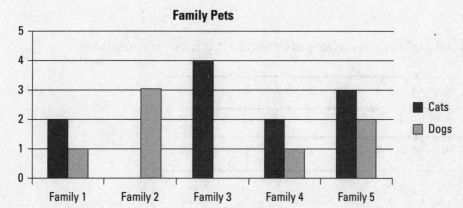

Family Pets

8. According to the chart, how many cats are kept as pets among the five families polled?

   (A) 4

   (B) 7

   (C) 9

   (D) 11

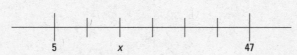

9. In the figure above, tick marks are equally spaced on the number line. What is the value of x?

   (A) 6

   (B) 17

   (C) 19

   (D) 25

10. If a and b are positive integers and $2^{3a} \times 2^{3b} = 64$, what is the value of $a + b$?

    (A) 1

    (B) $\dfrac{3}{2}$

    (C) 2

    (D) 4

11. If $\left(x - 4\right)^2 = 49$ and $x < 0$, what is the value of x?

    (A) −11

    (B) −5

    (C) −3

    (D) −1

Go on to next page

12. If $2a^2 = 56$, what is the value of $8a^2$?

(A) 144

(B) 156

(C) 212

(D) 224

13. In the *xy-coordinate* plane, the line with equation $y = 2x + 4$ crosses the *x*-axis at the point with coordinates (f, g). What is the value of *f*?

(A) –4

(B) –2

(C) 0

(D) 2

14. Which of the following represents all values of *x* that satisfy this inequality: $7 \geq -2x + 3$?

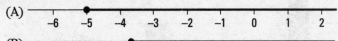

15. The figure above shows the graph of $y = f(x)$ from $x = -3$ to $x = 4$. For what value of *x* in this interval does the function *f* attain its minimum value?

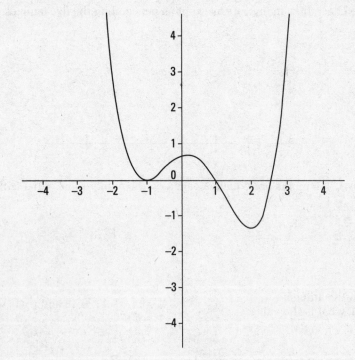

(A) 2

(B) 1

(C) 0

(D) –2

Go on to next page

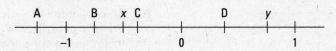

16. Which option best represents the product xy?

    (A) A

    (B) B

    (C) C

    (D) D

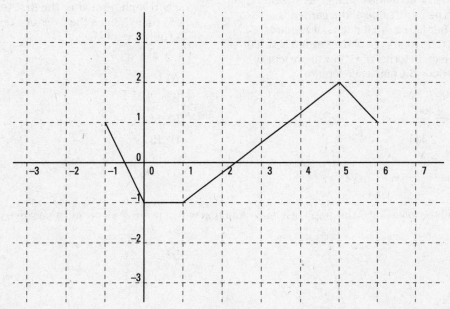

17. The graph of $y = f(x)$ is shown above. If $f(3) = ka$, which of the following could be the value of $f(k)$?

    (A) -1

    (B) $-\frac{1}{2}$

    (C) 0

    (D) $\frac{1}{2}$

18. If $-1 < x < 0$, which of the following statements must be true?

    I. $x > \frac{x}{2}$

    II. $x^2 > x$

    III. $x^3 > x^2$

    (A) I only

    (B) II only

    (C) I and II only

    (D) I, II, and III

Go on to next page

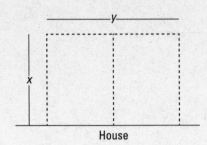

House

19. A gardener is building a fence to enclose her garden and divide it in half, as shown above. The fourth side of the garden is adjacent to her house, so it does not require fencing. The total area of the garden is 2,400 square feet. In terms of x, how many feet of fencing does the gardener require?

(A) $2,400 - 3x$

(B) $x + \dfrac{2,400}{x}$

(C) $3x + \dfrac{2,400}{x}$

(D) $3x + \dfrac{1,200}{x}$

20. An equilateral triangle has vertices at $(-1, 1)$ and $(5, 1)$. Which of the following might be the coordinates of the third vertex?

(A) $(2, -5)$

(B) $(2, 1 - 3\sqrt{3})$

(C) $(2, 3\sqrt{3})$

(D) $(3\sqrt{3}.1)$

21. In the following sequence, the first term is 2, and each term after the first term is 3 less than 3 times the previous term. What is the value of k?

2, 3, 6, k, 42

(A) 10

(B) 12

(C) 14

(D) 15

22. Which of the following is the graph of a linear function with a positive slope and a negative y-intercept?

(A)

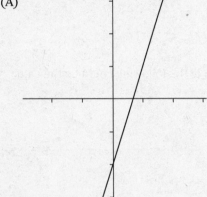

(C)

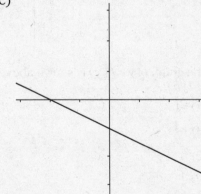

(B)

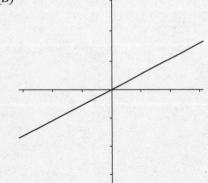

(D)

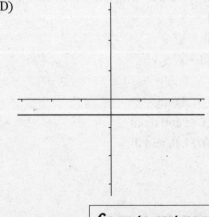

Go on to next page

23. A baker can bake three dozen cookies in 45 minutes. How many cookies can the baker make in one hour?

    (A) 4

    (B) 36

    (C) 40

    (D) 48

k	1	2	3	4	5	6
$f(k)$	15	11	7	n	−1	−5

24. The table above defines a linear function. What is the value of n?

    (A) 1

    (B) 2

    (C) 3

    (D) 4

25. When the number m is multiplied by 5, the result is the same as when 6 is subtracted from m. What is the value of $8m$?

    (A) −12

    (B) −6

    (C) $-\dfrac{3}{2}$

    (D) 3

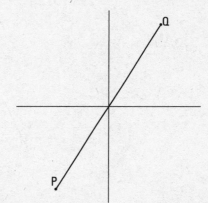

26. The coordinates of point P in the figure above are (a, b), where $|b| > |a|$. Which of the following could be the slope of PQ?

    (A) −3

    (B) $-\dfrac{1}{2}$

    (C) $\dfrac{1}{2}$

    (D) $\dfrac{3}{2}$

Go on to next page

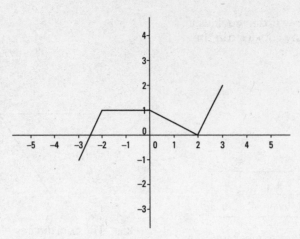

27. The graph of $y = g(x)$ is shown above. Which of the following could be the graph of $y = g(x - 1)$?

(A)

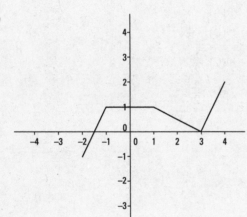

(C)

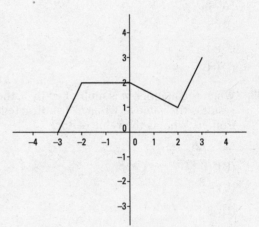

(B)

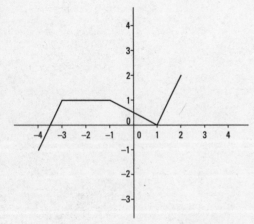

(D)

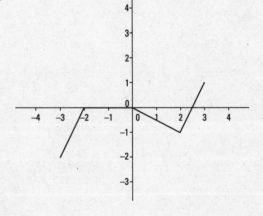

Go on to next page

28. In the *xy*-plane, lines *p* and *q* are perpendicular. If line *p* contains the points $(-2, 2)$ and $(2, 1)$, and line *q* contains the points $(-2, 4)$ and $(k, 0)$, what is the value of *k*?

    (A) –3

    (B) –2

    (C) –1

    (D) 0

29. If the arithmetic mean of 4, *p*, and *q* is 6, what is the value of $\frac{p+q}{2}$?

    (A) 2

    (B) 3

    (C) 6

    (D) 7

30. On a number line, 27 is exactly halfway between the point at 15 and another point. What is the value of the other point?

    (A) 12

    (B) 39

    (C) 51

    (D) 60

Directions for Questions 31–37: Solve the problem and then write your answer in the box provided on the answer sheet. Mark the ovals corresponding to the answer, as shown in the following example. Note the fraction line and the decimal points.

Write your answer in the box. You may start your answer in any column.

Although you do not have to write the solutions in the boxes, you do have to blacken the corresponding ovals. You should fill in the boxes to avoid confusion. Only the blackened ovals will be scored. The numbers in the boxes will not be read.

There are no negative answers.

Mixed numbers such as 31/2 may be gridded in as a decimal (3.5) or as a fraction (7/2). Do not grid in 3½. It will read as 31/2.

Grid in as a decimal as far as possible. Do not round your answer and leave some boxes empty.

A question may have more than one answer. Grid in only one answer.

Go on to next page

31. If $x^2 - y^2 = 39$ and $x - y = 3$, what is the value of y? [____]

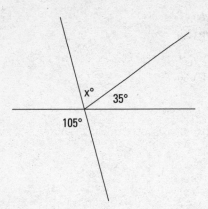

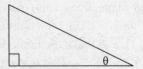

35. In the right triangle shown above, if angle $\theta = 30°$, what is sin θ? [____]

36. A circle lies in the *xy*-coordinate plane. The circle is centered at $(-3, 17)$ and touches the *y*-axis at one point only. What is the diameter of the circle? [____]

37. **Extended Thinking Question:** If \$1,000 invested at *i* percent simple annual interest yields \$200 over a two-year period, what dollar amount invested at the same rate will yield \$1,000 interest over a five-year period? Ignore the dollar sign when gridding your answer. [____]

32. What is the value of *x* in the figure above?
[____]

33. Six times a number is the same as the number added to 6. What is the number?
[____]

34. a, $a + 5$

The first term of the sequence above is *a*, and each term after the first is 5 greater than the preceding term. If the sum of the first six terms is 177, what is the value of *a*?
[____]

STOP DO NOT TURN THE PAGE UNTIL TOLD TO DO SO.
DO NOT RETURN TO A PREVIOUS TEST.

No-Calculator Section

Time: 25 minutes for 20 questions

Directions: This section contains two different types of questions. For Questions 1–15, choose the best answer to each question and darken the corresponding oval on the answer sheet. For Questions 16–20, follow the separate directions provided before those questions.

Notes:

✔ You may **not** use a calculator.

✔ All numbers used in this exam are real numbers.

✔ All figures lie in a plane.

✔ All figures may be assumed to be to scale unless the problem specifically indicates otherwise.

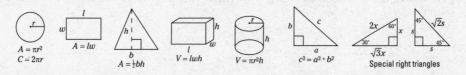

1. In the *xy*-coordinate plane, what is the area of the rectangle with opposite vertices at (–3, –1) and (3, 1)?

    (A) 3

    (B) 6

    (C) 9

    (D) 12

2. The following Venn diagram shows the ice-cream flavor choice of 36 children at an ice-cream party. Each child could choose vanilla ice cream, chocolate ice cream, both, or neither. What percent of the children had chocolate ice cream only?

    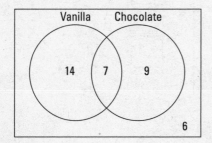

    (A) 10%

    (B) 25%

    (C) 50%

    (D) 75%

3. If $\frac{4}{5}$ of a number is 24, what is $\frac{1}{5}$ of the number?

    (A) 5

    (B) 6

    (C) 8

    (D) 18

Go on to next page

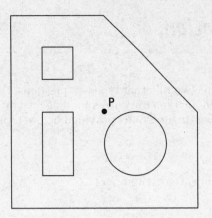

4. If the figure above were rotated 90 degrees clockwise about point *P*, which of the following would be the result?

(A)

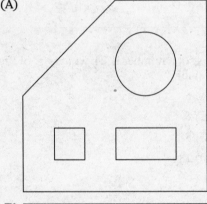

(C)

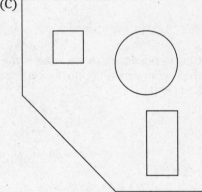

(B)

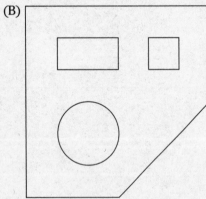

(D)

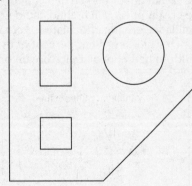

Go on to next page

5. Kate has been snowboarding for three fewer years than Chandler. If Chandler has been snowboarding for *n* years, which of the following expressions represents the number of years that Kate has been snowboarding?

    (A) $n-3$

    (B) $n+3$

    (C) $3-n$

    (D) $2n+3$

8. For all integers *n*, let $*(n)$ be defined by $*(n)=(n-1)(n+1)$. What is the value of $*(-3)$?

    (A) –9

    (B) –8

    (C) 3

    (D) 8

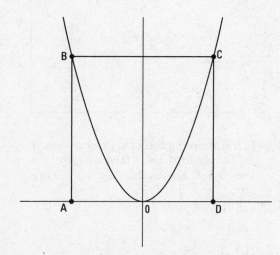

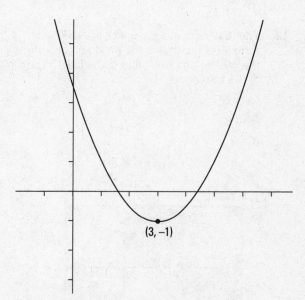

6. In the figure above, *ABCD* is a square and points *B*, *C*, and *O* lie on the graph of $y = \dfrac{x^2}{k}$, where *k* is a constant. If the area of the square is 36, what is the value of *k*?

    (A) 1.5

    (B) 3

    (C) 4.5

    (D) 6

9. In the parabola above, the vertex is at $(3,-1)$. Which of the following are *x*-coordinates of two points on this parabola whose *y*-coordinates are equal?

    (A) 1 and 5

    (B) 1 and 6

    (C) 2 and 5

    (D) 2 and 6

7. How much greater than $t-5$ is $t+2$?

    (A) 2

    (B) 4

    (C) 5

    (D) 7

10. The price of a television was first decreased by 10 percent and then increased by 20 percent. The final price was what percent of the initial price?

    (A) 88%

    (B) 90%

    (C) 98%

    (D) 108%

Go on to next page

11. In the *xy*-plane, the center of a circle has coordinates $(-2, 4)$. If one endpoint of a diameter of the circle is $(-2, 1)$, what are the coordinates of the other endpoint of this diameter?

    (A) $(-5, 4)$

    (B) $(-2, 6)$

    (C) $(-2, 7)$

    (D) $(1, 4)$

12. The first term of a sequence is –1. If each term after the first is the product of –3 and the preceding term, what is the fourth term of the sequence?

    (A) –27

    (B) –9

    (C) 9

    (D) 27

14. In the *xy*-plane, line *l* passes through $(-1, 3)$ and is parallel to the line $4x + 2y = k$. If line *l* passes through the point $(p, -p)$, what is the value of *p*?

    (A) –2

    (B) –1

    (C) 1

    (D) 2

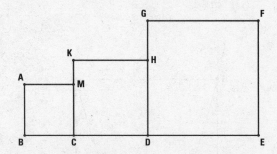

15. In the above figure, all shapes are squares, *BC* has length 4, and *CD* has length 7. Points *A*, *K*, and *G* all lie in the same line. Find the length of *DE*.

    (A) 10

    (B) 11

    (C) 11.5

    (D) 12.25

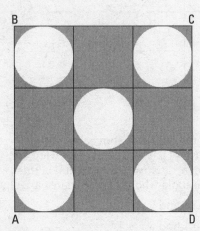

13. Square *ABCD* is divided into nine equal squares, five of which have circles inscribed in them. If $AB = 6$, what is the total shaded area?

    (A) $24 - 10\pi$

    (B) $24 - 5\pi$

    (C) $36 - 10\pi$

    (D) $36 - 5\pi$

Go on to next page

Directions for Questions 16–20: Solve the problem and then write your answer in the box provided on the answer sheet. Mark the ovals corresponding to the answer, as shown in the following example. Note the fraction line and the decimal points.

Answer: $^7/_2$

Answer: 3.25

Answer: 853

Write your answer in the box. You may start your answer in any column.

Although you do not have to write the solutions in the boxes, you do have to blacken the corresponding ovals. You should fill in the boxes to avoid confusion. Only the blackened ovals will be scored. The numbers in the boxes will not be read.

There are no negative answers.

Mixed numbers such as 31/2 may be gridded in as a decimal (3.5) or as a fraction (7/2). Do not grid in 3½. It will read as 31/2.

Grid in as a decimal as far as possible. Do not round your answer and leave some boxes empty.

A question may have more than one answer. Grid in only one answer.

16. Find the smallest even number that is divisible by 3, 5, and 7.

17. A certain fraction is equivalent to $\frac{2}{3}$. If the fraction's denominator is 12 less than twice its numerator, find the denominator of the fraction.

18. If $p > 0$ and $p^2 = 3p + 40$, what is the value of p?

19. A sequence of numbers begins 1, 5, 4, 8, 7, 11, 10. What is the 21st term of this sequence?

20. If $xy = 120$, and $\frac{1}{x} + \frac{1}{y} = \frac{1}{4}$, find $x + y$.

STOP DO NOT TURN THE PAGE UNTIL TOLD TO DO SO. DO NOT RETURN TO A PREVIOUS TEST.

Chapter 7

Answers and Explanations

• •

After you finish the practice test sections in Chapters 4, 5, and 6, take some time to go through the answers and explanations in this chapter to find out which questions you missed and why. Even if you answered the question correctly, the explanation might offer a useful strategy that speeds up your performance on the next round. We also include additional information that'll be useful on the real SAT. If you're short on time, turn to the end of this chapter to find an abbreviated answer key.

Answers for Section 1: Reading

1. **C.** Lines 3 through 4 state that "the absence of human landmarks is one of the most depressing and disheartening." Line 6 refers to "sod," or dirt, as "inescapable." "Inescapable," "depressing," and "disheartening" — all negative descriptions that apply to nature, in John Bergson's view. (Those words also apply to the SAT, by the way.) Did you select Choice (D) based on Line 34, which mentions Bergson's "Old-World belief that land, in itself, is desirable"? That statement comes in a paragraph that laments the pioneers' inability to farm the land "properly" (Line 36). In the same paragraph, Bergson compares the land to a "horse . . . that runs wild and kicks things to pieces" (Lines 35 through 36), clearly implying that land tamed by human efforts would be better.

2. **A.** Check out the explanation to Question 1. The land is "depressing and disheartening" because it lacks "human landmarks" (Lines 3 through 4). Choice (A) is the best evidence for the correct answer to Question 1.

3. **D.** Choices (A), (B), and (C) refer to natural features. Only Choice (D) describes something made by human beings. Though the roads are primitive — "faint tracks in the grass" (Line 7) — they are the result of human effort, or "strivings" (Line 10).

4. **C.** The first paragraph (Lines 1 through 10) shows a land that has been settled only on the most basic level. Because the "record of the plow was insignificant" (Lines 7 through 8), the reader imagines shallow marks in the soil, which are similar to scratches made ages ago by primitive, or "prehistoric" people. Thus, Choice (C) is correct.

5. **B.** The usual meaning of *genius* is "supersmart." In this passage, though, a less common definition fits "the spirit or character" of a place or person or time period.

6. **D.** The first four sentences of paragraph two (Lines 11 through 13) discuss the land in negative terms. Though Bergson had "come to tame" the land, he had not succeeded, because it was "still a wild thing" (Line 12) and cursed by bad luck ("Mischance" [Line 13]). True, Bergson is ill, but the paragraph isn't about his symptoms; it's about the land, making Choice (D) the best answer.

7. **A.** The third paragraph lists what went wrong on Bergson's farm: weather, a broken leg, snakebite, disease, and death. True, Bergson was unprepared for farming this land, as the last paragraph (Lines 34 through 40) reveals. However, simple bad luck dominates this paragraph, making Choice (A) the correct answer.

8. **B.** John Bergson had worked in a shipyard, and his neighbors were "tailors, locksmiths, joiners, cigar-makers" (Line 39). None of them were farmers. The land isn't the problem; the farmers are, because, to them, the land is an "enigma" (Line 35), or puzzle.

9. **D.** John Bergson has much to regret. The first paragraph (Lines 1 through 10) describes "depressing and disheartening" scenes. Lines 19 through 25 list the hardships Bergson endured, including the death of his animals, failure of his crops, and loss of two children to illness. After years on the homestead, John Bergson "had ended up pretty much where he began" (Line 27). Choice (D) fits nicely here, because the life you see in this passage is definitely not easy. A close second — but still incorrect answer — is Choice (A). Yes, Bergson was unprepared for the conditions in the New World (the logical term for his surroundings, as he left the "Old World" to go there). But he also faced bad luck (see the explanation to Questions 8). Therefore, Choice (A) is too extreme.

10. **C.** Reread the explanation to Question 9, and you see one bit of evidence — the hardships that Bergson endured — matches Choice (C). That's your answer!

11. **B.** The author quotes several ancient sources for information about the early Olympic games, the Olympiad. The quotations from Xenophanes (Line 1), Homer (Line 4), and Julius Africanus (Line 15) support the author's statements about the ancient games, providing evidence from people who witnessed them or who lived in ancient times and therefore were likely to know what they were talking — well, writing — about. These ancient commentators (like the experts on television during the modern games) have knowledge, and therefore, authority. As Choice (B) says, they *establish an authoritative voice.*

12. **A.** The figure accompanying this passage shows one spot — the Stadium Track — that is definitely for athletes. More space was allotted to administrative and religious structures, including the "treasuries," three altars, one temple, and a council house. Therefore, Choice (A) fits nicely here. Choice (B) is tempting, given the many religious references in the figure, but nothing in either the passage or the drawing proves that the Olympic area *was consecrated to the gods.* Choice (A) is correct.

13. **C.** The author compares the length of two races: the *stade,* the shortest race in ancient times (192.27 meters) and the 200-meter race of modern times. The modern race is nearly the same — the *realistic equivalent* of the older event.

14. **C.** Lines 13 through 14 tells you that "later Greeks found it convenient to use the sequence of Olympiads as a chronological reference" probably because the Olympics were "one of the few truly international institutions in Greece" (Line 13). Choice (C) works because it refers to *a common chronological reference point* — a measure of time for all states.

15. **D.** Take a look back to the explanation to Question 14, and you see that "later Greeks found it convenient to use the sequence of Olympiads as a chronological reference," as Choice (D) states.

16. **B.** Paragraph three (Lines 18 through 29) discusses running styles as depicted on ancient vases. The runners are compared to modern sprinters and long-distance racers. However, the author never mentions anything about himself. He may be a runner, but he may also be a couch potato who spends days watching athletic events on television. Choice (A) is a dud. Choice (C) doesn't work either, because you don't know when the vases were discovered — last week or centuries ago. Choice (D) is a nonstarter because all the evidence about running methods comes from vases, not from literature. You're left with Choice (B), which is a good bet because human anatomy *doesn't change.* Plus the paragraph devotes much attention to the way arms and legs move in each type of race. Arms and legs are parts of the body — human anatomy.

17. **A.** According to Line 27, "Ancient sources never specify the exact number of laps" and "modern opinions vary greatly" (Line 28). What do most historians think? The "most widely accepted" — *generally believed* — number is 20 laps. Choice (A) is your answer. Did you select Choice (C)? *To approve* is not the same as *to believe.* After all, a parent can *believe* that you blew off your homework but not *approve* of your actions!

18. **C.** In this passage, the author cites evidence from many sources, including vase paintings (Lines 19 through 20) and literature (Homer's Odyssey [Line xx]). He also quotes official documents (Hippias of Elis's catalogue of victors [Line 4]) and mentions archeological discoveries (the posthole at Nemea [Line 34]). Therefore, Choice (C) is correct. Choice (A) is clearly wrong because although the author frequently refers to historians, he also discusses areas of disagreement — such as how many turning posts were available to athletes in the ancient Olympics. *An accurate record of events* implies something that is settled and definitely true.

19. **D.** Scan the explanation to Question 18, and you see that the author refers to many types of evidence. Choice (D) provides reference to at least two, so it's the best choice here.

20. **C.** The athletes pictured on the vases might be either sprinters or long-distance runners. The author explains that "most scholars think" long-distance runners had to have their own turning posts to avoid "much congestion" (Line 38). However, the passage ends with speculation ("But if each . . . probably shows" [Lines 40 through 41]). So one turning post or many? Only *more research,* as Choice (C) says, will determine the answer.

21. **D.** As usual in a vocabulary-in-context question, all four answers are possible definitions of the word the test-makers are asking about. In context, though, only one choice fits. The 9 billion people who'll be living on Earth in 2050 will have a demand or "need" for food, making Choice (D) the best answer here.

22. **A.** Passage I argues for biodiversity in several spots. "Plant diversity has a critical role to play" in food and medicine, according to Line 9, and the world will lose "valuable **traits** [characteristics] and genes" (Line 16) and "knowledge, cultural traditions, and medicinal resources" (Line x) if biological diversity decreases. Passage I ends with a statement about "international experts" (Line 20) who want "a program for the conservation" of plants.

    Passage II goes even further, stating that if "biodiversity gets too low, then the future of life itself becomes threatened" (Lines 46 through 47). Passage II also calls protecting biodiversity "crucial" (Line 54) because doing so "increases the chance that at least some living things will survive in the face of large changes in the environment" (Lines 53 through 54). Sounds like *an argument in favor of biodiversity,* as Choice (A) states. The other choices represent information in the passages, but only Choice (A) applies to the main idea of both passages.

23. **D.** Check out the explanation to Question 22. Several lines support the fact that these passages argue for biodiversity. Only two of those lines appear in the answer choices, and they're in Choice (D), which is the correct answer.

24. **C.** Both passages make a strong case for biodiversity, as you see in the explanation for Question 22. Therefore, reliance on a small number of crops isn't a good idea, as Choice (C) indicates. Passage I states that plant diversity, a subcategory of biodiversity, "has a critical role to play in addressing the food and nutrition security and medicinal needs of the people of this world" (Lines 9 through 10). Passage II explains that biodiversity "increases the chance that at least some living things will survive in the face of large changes in the environment" (Lines 53 through 54). Choice (A) doesn't work because the author of Passage I sees exploitation as a fact of life for as long as the Earth has supported human life, not a negative factor. Choice (B) doesn't make the cut because the call for "a global program of conservation" (Line 36) implies that the rate of extinction can be slowed. Choice (D) drops out because Passage I doesn't address keystone species. Choice (C) is correct.

25. **C.** The passage refers to "an expected 9 billion people by 2050" (Line 3). In other words, that's the probable population of Earth in that year, as Choice (C) says. Did you select Choice (D)? Providing food for all of them may be a problem, because it's "unclear how our current global food system will cope" (Lines 4 through 5). However, the passage doesn't state that 9 billion will be undernourished, just that they will exist. Therefore, Choice (D) isn't correct.

26. **D.** Some areas have more biodiversity and some have less, according to Lines 12 through 13. The areas with more diversity tend to be in specific areas — where they are *grouped,* or concentrated, making Choice (D) the answer you seek.

27. **B.** Passage II tells you that when "mussels take over" (Line 51), other marine animals "disappear from the environment" (Line 52). In other words, the mussels *displace* or remove other species — as Choice (B) states. Choice (D) may have tempted you, but that answer is too extreme. You know only that the other species "disappear," not that they become extinct. They could be thriving in another spot! Choice (B) is the best answer here.

28. **C.** The graph tells you that the percentage of *undernourished persons* fell steadily from 1990 to 1992 (19 percent) to 2011 to 2013 (12 percent). Therefore, Statement I is true. According to Line x, more than 2 billion people *lack important nutrients,* but 868 million "suffer from hunger" (Line 4). Okay, Statement II works. Statement III falls apart because although the passage refers to an increasing rate of extinctions, you don't know whether the extinct species provided food for human beings. Because Statements I and II are true, the correct answer is Choice (C).

29. **A.** The statistics show that most of the world's food comes from a small number of plant species, so Choice (A) fits nicely here.

30. **C.** Passage II discusses keystone species, which are so important that their decline wrecks entire ecosystems. Though Passage II uses a marine environment to illustrate the need for healthy keystone populations, the principle can be transferred to other areas, such as forests. Choice (C) is the right one here.

31. **D.** When you compare passages, be sure that you understand the answer choices. Both passages deal with diversity in the environment, but Passage I focuses on diversity in food supplies — the opposite of the answer given in Choices (A) and (B). Passage I is about plants, again the opposite of Choice (C). Choice (D) is the winner here because Passage II discusses the relationships between species in an ecosystem.

32. **B.** During Lincoln's first inaugural speech, he set out plans for his presidency and for the nation "to be pursued" (Line 4) or followed. Now, however, he can't, because of "the great contest" — the war — that is still going on. Therefore, he can't make a *plan,* the best meaning of *course* in this context.

33. **C.** Lincoln states that "the progress of our arms" (Line 8) is "reasonably satisfactory and encouraging to all" (Line 9) and that there is "high hope for the future" (Line 10). Because he is speaking to his supporters, the pronoun *our* refers to those who agree with Lincoln — the Northern side of the conflict. What would be *satisfactory and encouraging?* Victory. Choice (C) is correct.

34. **D.** As you see in the explanation to Question 33, Lincoln finds "the progress of our arms" (Line 8) "reasonably satisfactory and encouraging to all" (Line 9).

35. **A.** Just before the statement that "little that is new could be presented" (Line 7), Lincoln speaks of "the great contest which still absorbs the attention, and engrosses the energies of the nation" (Lines 6 through 7). In other words, *the war monopolizes the attention and resources of the nation,* as Choice (A) says. Choice (B) doesn't work because in the last paragraph Lincoln sets forth a vision of the future, where he and others will "bind up the nation's wounds" (Line 45) and achieve "lasting peace among ourselves, and with all nations" (Lines 48 through 49). The passage contains no evidence for Choices (C) and (D).

36. **B.** Line 14 explains that during his first inaugural address, "insurgent agents were in the city" trying to "destroy" the Union "without war." These agents qualify as a *movement to disband the nation,* as Choice (B) states. Did you select Choice (C)? Lincoln carefully explains that neither side wanted war: "Both parties deprecated war" (Lines 15 through 16). However, both sides were willing to go to war if necessary. That last phrase — *if necessary* — tells you that support for war was not *unconditional.*

37. **C.** The third paragraph (Lines 18 through 23) discusses the issue of slavery, so Choice (B) is tempting. However, Lincoln — who strongly opposed slavery — discusses it as an "interest" that is powerful enough to cause the war. In fact, he says that to "strengthen, perpetuate, and extend this interest" the South was willing to go to war. So in this

context, Lincoln is using "interest" to describe the self-interest, or benefit, flowing to those who favored slavery.

38. **B.** Over and over, Lincoln looks for common ground: "Both parties deprecated war" (Lines 15 through 16), "Neither party expected" (Line 24), "Neither anticipated" (Line 25), "Each looked" (Line 26), "Both read" (Line 27), and so forth. Choice (B) works perfectly here.

39. **C.** The explanation to Question 38 lists several possible supporting points, one of which appears as Choice (C), which is your answer.

40. **D.** A quick glance at the fourth paragraph (Lines 24 through 31) shows that Lincoln sees common ideas between both Northerners and Southerners. (Check out the explanation for Question 38 for examples.) The last paragraph of the speech underlines the same point, setting out tasks that both sides must accomplish: "bind up the nation's wounds . . . care for him who shall have borne the battle, and for his widow, and his orphan" (Lines 45 through 46). Both sides have soldiers, widows, and orphans. The best proof, though, is in Line 47, where Lincoln calls for all to "achieve and cherish a just, and a lasting peace, among ourselves." Peace comes when warring sides — both Northerners and Southerners — stop fighting. No doubt about it: Choice (D) is the answer.

41. **C.** From the first words — "Fellow countrymen" (Line 1) — to the last — "peace among ourselves" (Line 47) — Lincoln focuses on the union of both North and South. True, he does condemn slavery, so Choice (B) is appealing. However, the discussion of slavery occurs in the context of the war. Many portions of the speech refer to the importance of preserving the Union ("saving the Union" [Line 13], for example) and the speech empha-sizes common ground between the warring sides, as in "he gives to both North and South" (Line 36). Therefore, Choice (C) is a better answer than Choice (B).

42. **B.** In several sentences, Lincoln refers to the Bible, sometimes with a direct quotation ("Woe unto the world" [Line 32]) and sometimes with an indirect allusion ("let us judge not" [Line 30]). Specific references to God also appear in the fourth, fifth, and sixth paragraphs. For these reasons, Choice (B) is best.

43. **D.** Many answer choices here, in typical SAT fashion, are definitions of *primary*. In the context of Line 1, however, only Choice (D) makes sense. Boil everything down to the essentials, and an eclipse occurs when something disappears.

44. **B.** The passage explains that if one thing is "covering over . . . something else" (Lines 1 through 2, you have an eclipse, as the "something else" disappears. If you place an apple in front of a grape, you can't see the grape from the front. The grape is *eclipsed*. Choice (B) fits the definition and is the correct answer.

45. **A.** The definition of an eclipse is "a disappearance, the covering over of something by something else" (Lines 1 through 2). The apple "covers" the grape and makes it disappear from view, so this line supports the answer to Question 44.

46. **A.** The passage begins with a definition of eclipse and moves on to the examples of eclipses of the sun and moon. You also see the definition of *plane* in Lines 21 through 22, not to mention definitions of *new* and *full* moons. Choice (A) is a clear winner here!

47. **C.** Line 7 asks the reader to imagine the Sun, Moon, and Earth arranged in a line. One of these is in the middle, and each of the other two is an "extreme" — the *outer* body. The diagram may help you with this one; it illustrates the position of the three bodies during an eclipse.

48. **C.** If you're a planetary scientist, this one is easy. You aren't? Never fear. Line 9 refers to "ever-moving bodies." Another clue: The sentence containing the words the question is asking about ("drawn between any two bodies at any given time" [Line 7]) begins with the word *consequently*. Right before *consequently,* you see *constantly in motion* (Line 6). Follow these clues, Sherlock, and you arrive at Choice (C).

49. **B.** In the explanation to Question 49, you see some lines that support Choice (C). One of those lines appears here, in Choice (B), which is your answer.

50. **D.** The Earth blocks the light of the Sun, casting a shadow on the Moon — the Earth's shadow, also known as Choice (D).

51. **C.** If the universe were flat — lying on a plane — there would be "in every year about 25 eclipses (of the sun and of the moon in nearly equal numbers)" — according to Lines 29 through 30. However, the passage explains that the Moon's orbit isn't on the same plane, so the three bodies line up much less frequently. The correct answer is Choice (C).

52. **B.** Lines 35 through 36 tells you that "eclipses of the Moon, when they occur, are visible over the whole hemisphere, or half, of the Earth." Eclipses of the Sun, however, are visible in "just a belt of the Earth no more than about 150 to 170 miles wide" (Line 37). Therefore, more people see eclipses of the Moon than of the Sun, as Choice (B) states. Did you fall for Choice (C)? The Sun, planets, and moons are in the solar system, but not other stars. You may know this fact from your science classes, but you don't need outside knowledge to rule out Choice (C). Just check Line 6, which defines the solar system as "the planets and their moons."

Answers for Section 2: Writing and Language

1. **C.** The original is a run-on sentence — that is, two complete sentences attached to each other by a comma — a huge no-no in the grammar world. Choices (B) and (D) correct the original problem, but Choice (B) adds *and,* resulting in a less mature expression. Choice (D) introduces a new mistake, changing the present-tense verb to past and breaking the pattern established in the paragraph, which is all in present tense. Choice (C) includes the necessary information in a grammatically correct way.

2. **B.** The sentence tells you that Molly's anxiety level should go down, because she is "nervously checking" and then, the vet hopes, she "can stand quietly." Okay, when you *subtract,* you do end up with a smaller number. However, anxiety isn't a number; it's a feeling. You can *lower* the intensity of a feeling, but you can't *subtract* it. Choice (B) is the word you seek here. Choice (C), by the way, is the opposite of what you want. Choice (D) establishes a level of importance — not what you need in this sentence.

3. **A.** The first paragraph focuses on one patient, Molly, and Dr. Virga's treatment of her. The second paragraph explains what an animal behaviorist does. By adding "He is an animal behaviorist," you establish a strong transition from paragraph one to paragraph two.

4. **D.** The original sentence has a list of activities that behaviorists study. Whenever you see a list, check that it's *parallel.* That's an English-teacher term for this rule: Everything doing the same job in the sentence must be in the same form. You have *eat, move, rest, play,* and, in the original, *relating.* Nope. Change *relating* to *relate* and read the list. Can you hear how everything matches? Now it's parallel and correct.

5. **C.** The sentence begins with a verb form, *identifying.* By the rules of grammar, the subject of the sentence must be doing the action expressed by an introductory verb form. The subject of the original sentence is *animals,* who are definitely not *identifying* problems. Switch the sentence around so that the behaviorist does the *identifying.* Both Choices (C) and (D) solve the problem. Choice (C) is better than Choice (D), though, because Choice (D) drags in an extra word, *they.*

6. **C.** Check the context of the underlined words. The sentence begins with *Even in this modern era.* Why include *now?* Both express the same idea, but only *now* is underlined. Delete *now,* and the sentence is fine.

7. **B.** When you place commas around a descriptive statement in a sentence, the commas act like little handles. You can lift out the words they surround and still say the same thing with just a bit less detail. In this sentence, though, removing *who has pets* changes the meaning of the sentence. Instead of talking about pet owners, you're talking about all people — *anyone.* To keep the intended meaning, dump the commas. Now you have to choose between Choices (B) and (D). *Anyone* is a singular pronoun. It must be matched with singular verbs. Choice (D) improperly introduces plural verbs *(have, see).* Go for Choice (B), and you're right.

8. **A.** *Elephants* is a plural word and should be matched with other plurals, as the original sentence does *(they see themselves).* This one needs no change, so Choice (A) is your answer.

9. **D.** If elephants recognize themselves in a mirror, they are self-aware, so the original makes no sense. *But* signals some sort of change, such as an exception to the first part of the sentence. However, you don't want to reverse course here; you want to continue, and the conjunction *and* fills the role nicely, making Choice (D) your answer.

10. **B.** Take a close look at the graph. The figure 11% comes from the projected increase in *all United States jobs of any type,* not jobs solely in the field of animal behavior. Now look at the number for *all animal behavior specialists.* The number there is 7%, so Choice (B) is correct.

11. **D.** You study more, and you make more money. That's the meaning of the last sentence, but *return* isn't the appropriate word in this context. Instead, the *higher paid careers reflect,* because they *show* the worth of *better education and training.* Choice (D) is the right answer.

12. **B.** The sentence focuses on a single point in the past, so simple past tense, *began,* is best here.

13. **B.** The underlined word describes *health,* not the wounded soldiers. Health may be *impaired* (weakened or damaged), but not *disabled.* That description, along with *unfit* and *wounded* — Choices (C) and (D) — may refer to people, but not to health.

14. **C.** The sentence establishes the topic of the paragraph: the trench system. Placed at the beginning of paragraph two, the topic sentence creates a link to the first paragraph, which is a general introduction to World War I, because the sentence mentions *World War I* and *the trench system.*

15. **D.** The three activities show up in a list in Choice (D), stated concisely and correctly. Choice (A) is a run-on sentence (two complete thoughts linked only by a comma, a grammatical crime). Choice (B) creates what English teachers call a misplaced modifier, because an introductory verb form *(Listening to the enemy)* must describe the subject of the sentence. In Choice (B), the *frontline trench* is *listening to the enemy* — not the intended meaning. Choice (C) is wordy and introduces a pronoun, *they,* without telling you who *they* are.

16. **A.** The frontline trenches, as the diagram and text make clear, were closest to the enemy. Behind those were the support trenches. The original sentence uses *backed by,* which tells the reader both the location and the function, because when you *back* something, you also provide support.

17. **B.** Check the figure. The communication trench isn't parallel to the others. How could it be when it was supposed to connect them? Parallel lines, like railroad tracks, never meet. Instead, the communication trench cuts across the other two, as you see in the figure.

18. **B.** The original sentence isn't a sentence at all. It's a fragment because it has no logical subject-verb pair. *The trenches laid* (the original wording) has the trenches placing themselves in the ground. Nope! Instead, *the trenches were laid* or *placed* by someone not named in the sentence.

19. **D.** The paragraph begins by telling the reader that the trenches *were not pleasant places,* but little else in the paragraph supports that statement except the information about the walls. Add Choice (D), and you have better evidence *(narrow, never quite dry).*

20. **C.** The underlined word, *they're,* means "they are" — not the meaning you want here. Opt for the possessive pronoun *their,* Choice (C), for a grammatically correct expression.

21. **A.** Choice (A) combines the sentence concisely, wasting no words. Choice (B) is concise, but it says too little. Choice (C) is wordy, and Choice (D) is wrong because it's a run-on sentence — two complete sentences can't be joined with just a comma.

22. **C.** The passage stops, but it has no real conclusion, so Choice (A) doesn't work. Choice (B) repeats information from the third sentence of the paragraph, and repetition is seldom a good idea. Choice (D) doesn't relate to the topic of the last paragraph and also repeats information from the first paragraph — two good reasons to reject it. The correct answer is Choice (C) because the sentence takes into account the topic of the last paragraph — the gap between civilians and soldiers — and also refers to "The Great War," an idea introduced in the first paragraph. By returning to this idea, the added sentence sums up the last paragraph and links the first and last paragraphs, giving a sense of unity to the passage.

23. **C.** The original sentence has no subject, so you have to add one. The rest of the passage is in first person — the narrator uses *I, me, my,* and so forth. It makes sense to add the subject *I.* In Choice (B), the *I* doesn't work as a subject because it doesn't pair with the verb form *sitting.* Choice (C), on the other hand, is a perfect match, because *I'm* is a contraction of *I am.* Choice (D) has no subject, so it fails. Go for Choice (C), which corrects the error.

24. **C.** The problem with the original is that *they've* (the contraction for *they have*) can have two meanings, because the pronoun *they* may refer to either *the Hamiltons* or the *parents.* The passage is clear: The parents have given in and gone to Vermont; the Hamiltons haven't given in and withdrawn their suggestion for a vacation spot.

25. **D.** The pronoun *which* refers to *dinner,* but Standard English requires the preposition *at,* because the family is *at the dinner.* Go for Choice (D).

26. **B.** The pronoun *everyone* is strange. It looks and sounds plural, but it's actually singular. (I know, grammar is dumb.) Because the next pronoun refers to *everyone,* it, too, must be singular, but *they* is plural. Change *they* to *he or she* (a singular, all-inclusive expression), and the pronouns match. Choice (B) is your answer.

27. **C.** Did you choose Choice (A)? If so, I fooled you with a common SAT trick. The original sentence is grammatically correct, but the SAT Writing and Language exam covers more than grammar. As written, the passage jumps from a memory of dinner with neighbors at home to greeting them in Vermont. The reader, with a little work, can figure out the meaning, but Choice (C) provides a transition to improve the flow from one idea to the next.

28. **C.** This question tests whether you can recognize or create focus in a paragraph. Most of the sentences deal with lake activities — swimming, boating, and fishing. Sentence 3 veers off course into the amount of vacation time the father has. Because it has no relation to the rest of the ideas in the paragraph, Sentence 3 has to go, and Choice (C) is your answer.

29. **D.** If the underlined words were an empty blank, what would you insert? Probably "like" or something similar. *Relish* means "enjoy." Choice (D) works in this context because the father doesn't like rowing. To *dote on,* by the way, means to act like a typical grandparent and to give way too much attention to something — not the word you need in the context of this sentence.

30. **A.** A *shard* is a small, sharp piece of something — the kind of thing that's leftover when you're cutting large chunks of marble. Even if you aren't acquainted with marble quarries, you can rule out the other choices. Choice (B) doesn't work because *columns* are finished products, and the end of the sentence indicates that the gift shop sells something *as well as* (in addition to) *finished items. Vestiges* are traces; you can't sell a trace! *Rubbles* isn't a word; the singular form, *rubble,* is the name for chunks of rock left after a building falls down. Choice (A), the original, is the only one that fits and is the correct answer.

31. **B.** The original wording is like someone who eats 4,000 calories a day and does nothing but sit on the couch and watch television. Diet time! When you slim down (in real life or in writing), you must do so carefully. Choice (B) conveys the correct meaning more concisely than the original. Choice (C) keeps the meaning, but it has to lose a few more pounds . . . er, I mean words. Choice (D) changes the meaning, because the *tombstones* aren't *nervous and glad* — the narrator is.

32. **C.** Why is the trip home so frightening? The paragraph supplies a little evidence: The narrator is worried that they will *drive into a ditch* or fail to find the cabin. Choice (C) adds more support for the fear expressed, explaining the reaction of *a city girl* to unlighted roads.

33. **D.** The tiny word *or* joins two statements, and by the rules of grammar, those statements must be parallel. In other words, they must match grammatically. Before *or,* you have a subject-verb statement — *that we'll drive off the road and into a ditch.* You have a subject (*we*) and a verb (*will drive,* when the contraction is removed). After the *or,* you need another subject-verb statement, which only Choice (D) supplies.

34. **D.** Commas surrounding a description make the description nonessential, or extra, to the meaning of the sentence. The original sentence identifies the rabbit-releaser by name. After you know the name, everything else — in this case, the fact that *Thomas Austin* was *an Australian* and someone *who enjoyed hunting* — is extra. The original sentence gets you halfway to the goal of correct punctuation by placing a comma after *hunting.* Halfway isn't good enough! Choice (D) isolates the description properly by inserting another comma after *Austin.*

35. **B.** The passage begins by explaining that *Thomas Austin . . . enjoyed hunting.* Why repeat the information? Delete this sentence, as Choice (B) indicates, and you create a more concise paragraph without sacrificing meaning.

36. **C.** In a sentence beginning with *there was* or *there were* (as well as *here was* or *here were*), the subject follows the verb. *There* (or *here*) can never be a subject. In this sentence, *some domestic rabbits* follows the verb. The subject, *rabbits,* is plural, so you need the plural verb *were.* Why Choice (C) and not Choice (D)? *Their* is a possessive pronoun, and the meaning of the sentence has nothing to do with possession.

37. **D.** Choice (D) is the most concise, yet it conveys the same information as the original. The other choices aren't incorrect, but they are all wordy.

38. **B.** This question tests you on two word pairs: less/fewer and led/lead. *Less* applies to quantities that you can measure but not count (*sand,* for example). *Fewer* is for counting things, such as *trees. Led* is the past tense form of the verb *to lead. Lead* is the present tense form (not what you need here) or, as a noun, a metal. *Fewer trees led,* Choice (B), is correct,

39. **A.** Don't mess with Mother Nature! That's what you do in an *interference,* a word that's correct in this context. Time to build your vocabulary: An *intercession* takes place when one pleads on behalf of another. (Don't confuse this word with *intersession,* which is a period of time between school semesters.) An *interruption* stops the flow of activity, and an *affectation* is a pretense or artificial expression. None of the other choices fit, so Choice (A) is your answer.

40. **B.** The original paragraph tells you little about why the beetles were introduced into the environment. When you add the information in Choice (B), the paragraph makes more sense.

41. **D.** The usual meaning of *introduce* is to bring two strangers together (*Alice, this is George.*) In this context, the strangers are a species (the tamarisk beetle) and an ecosystem. *To initiate* (the original word), as well as *to start* and *to commence,* is to begin something new. None of these words fits the context.

42. **C.** *The number of* is a singular subject referring to a single number, no matter how big that number is. Therefore, you have to pair this singular expression with a singular verb, *has decreased.* Choice (C) is correct here.

43. **B.** The original is wordy. Choice (B) puts the original on a diet and slims it down correctly. True, Choice (D) is even shorter, but it leaves the sentence without a subject and isn't Standard English.

44. **C.** Choice (C) adds specific examples to the more general original *(You should also check consumption),* which also inappropriately shifts from third person (talking about the subject) to second person (talking to the reader). The examples strengthen the writer's recommendation — that human interaction with nature should be accomplished carefully. Choices (A) and (D) are too general, and Choice (B) is repetitive. No doubt about it, Choice (C) is best.

The Essay

Here are some possible points to make in your essay in response to the prompt in Chapter 5:

- The main argument is that everyone gives "messages" to others, either through words or body language and facial expression. Positive messages create positive results, and negative messages do the opposite.

- The passage begins with a reference to the views of an expert witness, Paul Ekman. Although Ekman's credentials don't appear in the passage, the implication is that the book is an authoritative source.

- Immediately after the reference to Ekman, the author elaborates on the main point by explaining that even unconscious lies have an effect on the listener.

- At the end of paragraph one, the author appeals to fear by warning: "Others may subconsciously notice the disconnection between your words and your nonverbal message" and sense the lie.

- The example of Viktor Frankl in paragraph two contrasts Frankl's honesty ("unity between his words, his actions, and the way he lived") with the warning about lying at the end of paragraph one. Also countering the fear are the recommendations in paragraphs six and seven, which suggest positive messages the reader can give to him- or herself and to others. The passage ends with a practical method — a journal exercise — for nurturing a positive attitude.

- Personal pronouns — *we* and *you* (as in *We all know* and *What are you communicating to yourself*) create a bond between the author and reader.

- In the third and fourth paragraphs, a series of rhetorical questions (asked for effect, with no answer from the author) draw the reader into the discussion and provoke reflection on the topic.

- Sophisticated vocabulary choices, such as *executive, aligned*, and *congruent,* create a serious, businesslike tone. These words imply that the reader (even one who has to look up the definitions!) is serious and businesslike. That impression, flattery or not, may make the reader more open to the writer's argument.

- The research experiment on teachers' attitudes and the information about placebos discussed in paragraphs five and six provide scientific backing for the author's ideas.

- The conclusion refers to "meaning in life" and unifies the passage by taking the reader back to the example of Viktor Frankl.

- The conclusion also reinforces the main idea, that one can achieve greater "happiness, self-esteem, and effectiveness."

Answers for Section 3: Math

Calculator section

1. **C.** You know that three marbles are green and six are yellow, so nine of the marbles are already accounted for. That leaves $11 - 9 = 2$ red marbles in the box. The probability of drawing a red marble is the number of red marbles divided by the number of marbles in the box, or $\frac{2}{11}$, Choice (C).

2. **D.** You know that Car C is traveling at 60 miles per hour. Because Car C is going 20 miles per hour faster than Car B, you can determine that Car B is traveling 40 miles per hour ($60 - 20 = 40$). Finally, because Car A is traveling twice as fast as Car B, Car A's speed is $2 \times 40 = 80$ miles per hour.

3. **D.** Because no two points on the correct graph have the same y-coordinate, you know that for any y-value you pick, a horizontal line drawn at that y-value will cross the graph only once. The only option where that is true is Choice (D) because all of the other answers have parts where a horizontal line could cross the graph more than once.

4. **C.** For problems like this, your best bet is to follow the rule given and use substitution. You can see that 6 is in the place of a, 3 is in the place of b, and 4 is in the place of c. That means that you can change $a^2 - bc + b$ into $(6)^2 - (3)(4) + (3)$, which you can then simplify to $36 - 12 + 3 = 27$.

5. **C.** Call the unknown number in the question x. You know that 3 less than twice x is 13. Turning that into math: $2x - 3 = 15$. You can solve that equation by adding 3 to both sides and then dividing by 2 to get $x = 8$. Make sure that you don't get fooled here and think that 8 is the answer! The question asks for what five times the number (x) is, so $5x = 5(8) = 40$, Choice (C).

6. **B.** In this problem, you need to remember that 25 percent of something is a quarter. Because you're looking for which pizza toppings represent more than a quarter of total sales, you're looking for toppings that take up more than a quarter of the circle. Keep in mind that a quarter of a circle has a central angle of 90 degrees, so any central angle that is bigger than 90 degrees is part of a sector that is more than 25 percent. Pepperoni and Mushroom seem to be the only toppings that take up more than a quarter, so your answer is *two*, Choice (B).

7. **D.** A great idea here is to simply plug in the answer choices and see which one works out. When you plug in 0, Choice (A), you quickly see that $|10 - 3(0)| = |10 - 0| = 10$, which is bigger than 3. Plugging in 1, you end up with 7, which is also bigger than 3. Plug in 2, and the result is 4, which is still bigger than 3 (though you're getting closer!). Now try plugging in 3: $|10 - 3(3)| = |10 - 9| = 1$, and $1 < 3$! Choice (D) must be the right answer.

8. **D.** First, read the chart and determine how many cats each family has. Cats are indicated by the darker bars on the chart, so Family 1 has two cats, Family 2 has no cats (only dogs), Family 3 has four cats, Family 4 has two cats, and Family 5 has three cats. Add all of the cats together: $2 + 0 + 4 + 2 + 3 = 11$. There are 11 pet cats among these five families.

9. **C.** Count the spaces between the 5 and the 47. There are six spaces that are 42 apart (because $47 - 5 = 42$). Because the spaces are all the same size, you can find the length of each space by dividing 42 into 6, for a space length of 7. The unknown number is two spaces away from 5, so if each space is 7, find x by adding 2×7 to 5: $2(7) + 5 = 19$ for an answer of 19.

10. **C.** Here's a problem where you need to remember the rules of exponents. Do you recall that $x^a \cdot x^b = x^{a+b}$? That means that, in this case, you can simplify: $2^{3a} \cdot 2^{3b} = 2^{3a+3b}$. Hopefully you also saw that 64 is a power of $2 - 2^6$ to be exact. Rewriting the equation gives you $2^{3a+3b} = 2^6$. Since the base is the same on each side, 2, you can set the powers

equal to each other so that $3a + 3b = 6$. You're looking for the value of $a + b$, so divide both sides by 3 and you get that $a + b = 2$, Choice (C).

11. **C.** For this problem, you could always just plug in the answer choices to find one that works, or you can see that because $(x - 4)^2 = 49$, you're looking for when $x - 4 = 7$ or -7. The problem states that $x < 0$, so solve the $x - 4 = -7$ equation and discover that $x = -3$.

12. **D.** You know that $2a^2 = 56$, and you're looking for $8a^2$, which is $4(2a^2) = 4(56) = 224$.

13. **B.** When a line crosses the x-axis, you know that the y-value at that point has to be 0. That means you can plug 0 into the equation for y and solve for the x:

$$0 = 2x + 4$$
$$-4 = 2x$$
$$x = -2$$

The key to this problem is remembering that when you're thinking about an x-intercept, the y-value is 0. Don't forget that it's also true that when you're working with y-intercepts, the x-value is 0.

14. **B.** The key to this problem is remembering that when you multiply or divide an inequality by a negative number, the inequality switches. For example: Subtract 3 from both sides of the original expression $7 \geq -2x + 3$ to get $4 \geq -2x$. Then divide both sides by -2 (remember to switch the inequality sign!), and you end up with $-2 \leq x$ or $x \geq -2$.

So you're looking for a number line that includes values that are greater than or equal to -2. Only Choices (B) and (D) have the number line shaded in for numbers greater than or equal -2. Choice (B) has the circle at -2 filled in, meaning that -2 is included in the solution set, which is exactly what you want because you're looking for all numbers greater than or *equal to* -2.

15. **A.** The minimum value of a function is where the y-value is the lowest. So looking at the graph in this question, the y-value looks the lowest to the right of the y-axis, where the x's are positive. That already eliminates Choice (D). When you're trying to determine *where* the minimum value is, you need to find the x-value that causes the function to have the lowest y-value. Looking at the graph, the lowest y-value occurs when x is 2, Choice (A).

16. **C.** This problem is much easier if you pick numbers for x and y. For example, you could say that x is at about -0.5 and that y is at about 0.75 on the number line. When you multiply those two numbers together, you get $(-0.5)(0.75) = -0.375$. Because you're looking for a negative number, you can already disregard Choice (D); it represents a positive number. Similarly, Choice (A) is smaller than -1, so it's outside of the range of numbers that you're interested in. You're left with Choices (B) and (C). When you multiply a number by a number between 0 and 1, the number will get smaller (closer to 0). Therefore, when you multiply x by y, the answer is going to be closer to 0 than x is. That means that Choice (C) is your best bet.

17. **A.** If you look at the graph, you can figure out what k is. The question tells you that $f(3)$ represents the y-value on the graph when the x-value is 3. If you look on the graph, when x is 3, you can see that y is $\frac{1}{2}$, so you know that $k = \frac{1}{2}$. Now, $f(k) = f\left(\frac{1}{2}\right)$, so you're looking for the y-value when x is $\frac{1}{2}$. Check out the graph again, and you'll see that when x is $\frac{1}{2}$, y is -1.

18. **B.** This problem is easiest if you pick a number for x. One number that would work is $x = -0.5 = -\frac{1}{2}$. So now you want to test each of the statements out. Is $-0.5 > \frac{-0.5}{2}$?

Simplifying, is $-0.5 > -0.25$? That's clearly not true, so Statement I is false, meaning that you can eliminate Choices (A) and (C). Choices (B) and (D) both claim that Statement II is true, so you need to check Statement III to decide which answer choice is best. Statement III says that $(-0.5)^3 > (-0.5)^2$? Using a calculator, you can simplify this inequality to $-0.125 > 0.25$, which lets you see that it's clearly not true. Because Statement III is false, Choice (B) is the best choice. You can check Statement II to make sure: Is $(-0.5)^2 > (-0.5)$? Simplifying, you get $0.25 > -0.5$, which is absolutely true. Choice (B) really is the correct answer.

19. **C.** You can see that the fence the gardener will need is equal to $3x + y$, so what you really need to do is figure out a way to represent y in terms of x. The problem tells you that the area of the garden is 2,400 square feet, so you can use your knowledge of the area of a rectangle to see that $2,400 = xy$. Divide both sides by x to solve for y, which gives you $y = \dfrac{2,400}{x}$, and then you can substitute that back in to the original expression for the total fencing needed: $3x + y = 3x + \dfrac{2,400}{x}$, Choice (C).

20. **B.** To help solve this problem, sketch a picture. Keep in mind that the triangle can point upward or downward.

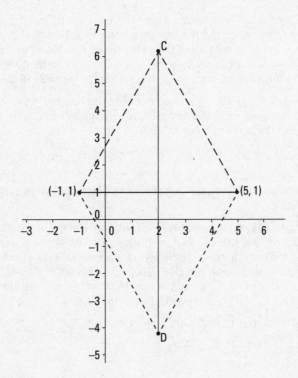

The third vertex of the triangle will lie along the line that cuts through the midpoint between the two given vertices. You can find the coordinates of that midpoint by finding the average of the x's and the average of the y's: $\left(\dfrac{-1+5}{2}, \dfrac{1+1}{2}\right) = (2,1)$. So the x-coordinate of the third vertex will be 2, which eliminates Choice (D). Because equilateral triangles have 60-degree angles in them, you can drop an altitude from the unknown vertex to make a 30-60-90 triangle. You know that the leg connecting a vertex to the midpoint is going to be 3 units long, and from there, you can use your knowledge of special triangles to see that the unknown altitude is $3\sqrt{3}$. That means that the unknown vertex is $3\sqrt{3}$ away from $(2,1)$, so it's either at $\left(2, 1+3\sqrt{3}\right)$ or $\left(2, 1-3\sqrt{3}\right)$. Choice (B) is the only choice that fits.

21. **D.** You're looking for the term that comes after 6. Because each term is three less than three times the previous term, you have to multiply 6 by 3 and then subtract 3: $6(3) - 3 = 18 - 3 = 15$. You can then check that 15 is the right answer by making sure that 42 would be the next term: $15(3) - 3 = 45 - 3 = 42$. That works, so you know that k is 15, and the answer is Choice (D).

22. **A.** For this problem, remember that a line with a positive slope looks like it's traveling uphill as you read it from left to right. Choices (A) and (B) are the only two that look like they have positive slope; Choice (C) has a negative slope (travel downhill as you read left to right); and Choice (D) has a slope of zero. Now you're looking for the option with a negative y-intercept. The y-axis is the vertical one, so you're looking for the option where the line hits the vertical axis below the origin. Choice (A) is the only option that satisfies both the requirement for positive slope and the requirement for a negative y-intercept. In case you're wondering, Choice (C) also has a negative y-intercept, but as you saw earlier, the slope is negative.

23. **D.** If a baker bakes three dozen cookies in 45 minutes, you can deduce that the baker bakes one dozen cookies in 15 minutes. Because you want to know how many cookies are made in an hour (60 minutes), you multiply by 4 and get 4×1 dozen $= 4$ dozen cookies. One dozen equals 12, so in one hour, the baker can make $4 \times 12 = 48$ cookies.

24. **C.** Looking at the chart, you can see that the top row increases by one in each box. In the bottom row, each box is four fewer than the previous one. That means that n will be four fewer than 7, or n is $7 - 4 = 3$.

25. **A.** For this problem, you want to set up an equation. The problem says that when m is multiplied by 5, the result is the same as when 6 is subtracted from m. Translating that into math: $5m = m - 6$. Gather all of the m terms on one side. Now you can solve for m and then determine what $8m$ equals, or you can go multiply both sides of this equation by 2 to go straight to the answer, because $2(4m) = 8m$: $2(4m) = 2(-6) = -12$.

26. **D.** Looking at the picture, you can see that the line has a positive slope (as you read left to right, the line goes up). Already you can eliminate Choices (A) and (B). To find the slope of the line, use the points (a, b) and $(0,0)$:

$$m = \frac{b-0}{a-0} = \frac{b}{a}$$

You know from $|b| > |a|$ that the fraction will be larger than 1, making Choice (D) the only viable choice.

27. **A.** When you change the x-value in a function, the graph changes horizontally. In this case, you're subtracting 1 from x before plugging it into the function g, so the graph shifts either left or right. Knowing this narrows your choices down to Choices (A) and (B). You can look at the original graph and see that $g(2) = 0$. To get $y = g(x - 1)$ to equal 0, you need $x - 1$ to equal 2: $x - 1 = 2$, $x = 3$. That means that $(3, 0)$ will be a point on the transformed graph. Choice (A) is the only graph with that point on it.

28. **A.** Your first step is to find the slope of line p.

$$m = \frac{2-1}{-2-2} = \frac{1}{-4} = -\frac{1}{4}$$

You know that perpendicular lines have opposite (negative) reciprocal slopes, so the slope of line q must be 4. So far, you know that line q has a slope of 4 and passes through the point $(-2, 4)$. You can use the equation $y = 4x + 12$ and substitute the point in to figure out what b is: $4 = 4(-2) + b$ becomes $b = 12$ when you solve it. Now you have the equation of line q: $(-2, 4)$. Substitute in the point $(k, 0)$ and solve for k: $0 = 4k + 12$, $-12 = 4k$, and $k = -3$.

29. **D.** To find the arithmetic mean (the average) of a set of numbers, you simply add the numbers together and then divide by the number of numbers. That means that if the average of 4, p, and q is 6, then $\frac{4+p+q}{3} = 6$. You can manipulate this equation by multiplying both sides by 3 $(4 + p + q = 18)$ and then subtracting 4 from both sides: $p + q = 14$. You're looking for the value of $\frac{p+q}{2}$, so just divide 14 by 2 and get 7.

30. **B.** There are two good ways to solve this problem. The easy way is to figure out that 27 and 15 are 12 units away from each other, and then simply add 12 to 27 to get the other

point, 39. Alternatively, you can use the idea that the average of 15 and the other point, x, is 27. Set that up like this:

$$\frac{15+x}{2}=27$$

After you multiply both sides by 2 and then subtract 15, you get that x is 39.

31. **5.** For this problem, you need to factor a difference of perfect squares: $x^2-y^2=(x-y)(x+y)$. Substitute in the numbers that you know, $39=(3)(x+y)$, and then divide both sides by 3 to get $x+y=13$. Because you know both $x+y$ and $x-y$, you can add the two together: $(x+y)+(x-y)=2x=13+3=16$. Now you know that x is 8. If x is 8 and $x+y=13$, y is 5.

32. **70.** The trick is to see that $105°$ is a vertical angle to $35°+x°$. Because vertical angles are equal, you know that $105=35+x$, so $x=70$.

33. **1.2 or 6/5.** Call the number x. Translating the words into math: "Six times x is the same as x added to 6" becomes $6x=6+x$. You can then gather all of the x terms onto one side of the equation, $5x=6$, and divide by 5: $x=\frac{6}{5}=1.2$.

34. **17.** First, start by listing out each of the terms: a, $a+5$, $a+10$, $a+15$, $a+20$, and $a+25$. Now add all six terms together: $a+a+5+a+10+a+15+a+20+a+25=6a+75$. You can set that equal to 177 and then solve for a:

$$6a+75=177$$
$$6a=102$$
$$a=17$$

35. **1/2 or 0.5.** If one angle is $90°$ and angle $\theta=30°$, then the third angle is $60°$, making this a 30-60-90 triangle with a side ratio of $1:\sqrt{3}:2$. The sin of an angle is the angle's opposite side, which in this case the triangle's smallest side, over the triangle's hypotenuse. From the ratio, you know that the smallest side is half the length of the hypotenuse, for an answer of $\frac{1}{2}$ or 0.5. When you grid in your answer, either 1/2 or 0.5 is considered correct.

36. **6.** Sketch out the problem to help you solve:

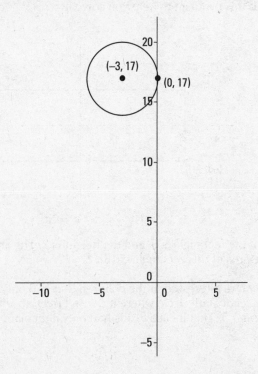

You can quickly see that for the circle to touch the *y*-axis in only one place, it must touch the *y*-axis at (0, 17). That point is three units away from the center of the circle, meaning that the radius of the circle is 3. Now just multiply that by 2 to determine the diameter of the circle is 6.

37. **2,000.** If $1,000 invested at *i* percent simple annual interest yields $200 over a two-year period, you can deduce that it earns $100 over one year. To find *i*, the interest rate, yielding $100 simple annual interest on $1,000, divide the amount of interest by the amount of the investment:

$$\frac{100}{1,000} = 0.1 = 10\%$$

Knowing the interest rate is 10 percent, how much should be invested at 10 percent for five years to yield $1,000? Because $1,000 over five years is $200 per year, you can set the equation up for one year's worth of interest with *x* as the investment and 10 percent as the interest rate:

$$10\%x = \$200$$
$$\frac{10x}{100} = \$200$$
$$\frac{x}{10} = \$200$$
$$x = \$2,000$$

At 10 percent simple annual interest, a $2,000 investment will yield $200 per year and $1,000 over five years.

No-calculator section

1. **D.** Sketch out this problem to help you solve it:

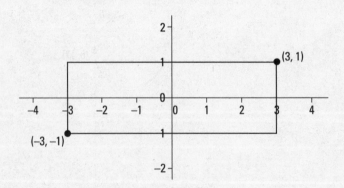

The length of the rectangle is 6, and the height is 2. The area of a rectangle is *length* times *width,* so the area of this rectangle is $(6)(2) = 12$.

2. **B.** Because you're interested in the children that had only chocolate ice cream, you want to look in the chocolate circle where it doesn't overlap with the vanilla circle; the number in that section is 9. That means 9 kids had only chocolate ice cream, out of the 36 kids at

the party. To find the percent of children who had chocolate ice cream, simply divide the part that you're interested in (9) by the whole (36):

$$\frac{9}{36} = \frac{1}{4} = 25\%$$

3. **B.** Set up the equation with x as the number and solve for x.

$$\frac{4}{5}x = 24$$
$$4x = 120$$
$$x = 30$$

Now find $\frac{1}{5}$ of 30, which is 6.

4. **B.** The best way to do this problem is to simply turn the test booklet. Look at the original image after turning the booklet 90 degrees clockwise (to the right), and then find the answer that looks most like the original did when it was turned. Choice (B) turns out to be the right one.

5. **A.** A good method for solving this one is to pick numbers for the variable. You could say, for example, that Chandler has been snowboarding for ten years — now you're using $n = 10$. If Kate has been snowboarding for three fewer years than Chandler, she has been snowboarding for 7 years. So you're looking for an answer choice where if you plug in $n = 10$, you get 7 as the result. Choice (A) works perfectly.

6. **A.** The key to this problem is paying attention to the fact that the figure is a square. Knowing that the area is 36, you can immediately deduce that the length of a side of the square is 6 because $6^2 = 36$. You also know that the length of half the side of the square is 3. That means that the (x, y) coordinates of point C will be $(3, 6)$. You can then plug those coordinates into the equation $y = \frac{x^2}{k}$ and solve for k:

$$6 = \frac{3^2}{k}$$
$$6 = \frac{9}{k}$$
$$6k = 9$$
$$k = \frac{3}{2} \text{ or } 1.5$$

7. **D.** Get rid of the t, and the question becomes, "How much greater than –5 is 2?" Well, that would be 7, so Choice (D) is the right answer.

8. **D.** You want to use substitution to solve this problem. Wherever you see n in the original definition, substitute in –3: $(n-1)(n+1) = (-3-1)(-3-1) = (-4)(-2) = 8$. Choice (D) is the best answer.

9. **A.** The key to this problem is remembering that parabolas are symmetric along the line that passes vertically through the vertex (known as the *axis of symmetry*). That means that if you were to fold the parabola along that line, both sides would line up. For the purpose of this problem, it means that x-values with the same y-coordinates must be the same distance from the axis of symmetry, which is at $x = 3$ in this case. Both values in Choice (A) are two away from 3, so that looks like a great option. In Choice (B), 1 is two away from 3, but 6 is three away, so that option doesn't work. For Choice (C), 2 is one away from 3, but 5 is two away; again they're not the same distance from the axis of symmetry. Choice (D) keeps 2, which is still one away from 3, and moves the other point further away, to 6. Choice (A) it is!

10. **D.** Whenever you're working on percentage problems, it's a great idea to assume that the starting price is $100. So if the TV cost $100 to start, and then the price was decreased by 10 percent ($10), the reduced price is $90. You add 20 percent on to 90 by finding 20 percent of 90 and adding it to $90: $0.20(90) = 18$; $90 + $18 = 108. It's easy to see that $108 is 108 percent of $100: $\frac{\$108}{\$100} = 1.08 = 108\%$.

11. **C.** It's always a great idea to sketch problems where you're told the coordinates but not given a picture.

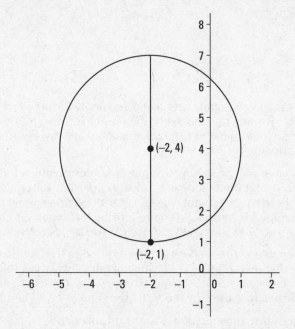

Looking at your picture, it's easy to see that the other endpoint of the diameter is also going to have –2 as its x-coordinate. Now all you need to do is determine the radius of the circle so you can figure out the y-coordinate. Looking at the two points that were given in the problem, you can see that the radius is 3 ($4 - 1 = 3$). That means that the y-coordinate of the other endpoint will be 3 away from the center: $(-2, 4 + 3) = (-2, 7)$.

12. **D.** For this problem, it's a good idea to just calculate each of the terms. You know that the first term is –1. To get the second term, multiply –1 by –3: $(-1)(-3) = 3$. To get the third term, multiply the second term by –3: $(3)(-3) = -9$. For the fourth term, multiply the third term by –3: $(-9)(-3) = 27$. Therefore the fourth term is 27, Choice (D).

13. **D.** The first step is to find the area of square *ABCD*. You know the length of one of the sides, so you know that the area is that length squared: $6^2 = 36$. Now you just need to subtract off the area of the five circles. You can see that each of the nine smaller squares has a side length equal to 1/3 of the length of the big square: $\frac{1}{3}(6) = 2$. That means that the diameter of each of the circles is 2, so the radius is 1. The area of a circle is $A = \pi r^2$, so the area of each of these circles is $A = \pi(1)^2 = \pi$. Now you can find the area of the shaded part of the diagram. The area will be the total square area minus the area of five circles: $36 - 5\pi$, or Choice (D).

14. **C.** The first step is to find the slope of the given line by solving for y:

$$2y = -4x + k$$

$$y = -2x + \frac{k}{2}$$

The slope of this line is –2. Because you know that line *l* is parallel to this line, you now know that line *l* has a slope of –2. Now you can use the point $(-1, 3)$ and $y = mx + b$ to determine the equation of l. Substitute -2 for m, -1 in for x, and 3 in for y, and then solve for b: $3 = -2(-1) + b$, so $b = 1$. Now you know the equation for l is $y = -2x + 1$. You can substitute p and $-p$ in for x and y, respectively, to solve the problem: $-p = -2(p) + 1$. Simplifying, $-p = -2p + 1$, or $p = 1$.

15. **D.** This is a tricky question! It's a good idea to sketch some axes in on the diagram so you can play with coordinates. You might choose to sketch them in so that the origin is at the lower left corner of the smallest square, like so:

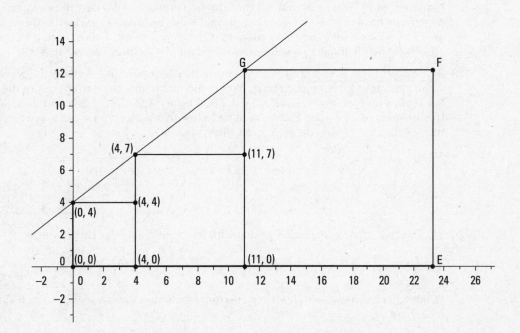

Now you can call point A $(0, 4)$ and point K $(4, 7)$. Because you have two points, you can determine the equation of the line passing through them (and through point G). The slope is

$m = \dfrac{7 - 4}{4 - 0} = \dfrac{3}{4}$. You already know the y-intercept is 4, so the equation of the line is $y = \dfrac{3}{4}x + 4$.

To figure out the coordinates of point G, you just need to plug the known x-value ($4 + 7 = 11$) into the equation of the line:

$$y = \frac{3}{4}(11) + 4 = \frac{33}{4} + \frac{16}{4} = \frac{49}{4} = 12\frac{1}{4} = 12.25$$

Therefore, the coordinates of point G are $(11, 12.25)$. Because you set the axes up so that the square was sitting on the x-axis, the y-coordinate of point G is equal to the length of a side of the largest square. DE is just another side of the same square, so the length of DE is also 12.25, Choice (D).

16. **210.** Every even number must be divisible by 2, so $2 \times 3 \times 5 \times 7 = 210$.

17. **36.** If you let the numerator equal n, then the denominator is $2n - 12$; thus,

$$\frac{2}{3} = \frac{n}{2n - 12}$$

So $2(2n - 12) = 3n$, or $4n - 24 = 3n$. Subtracting $4n$ from both sides gives you $-24 = -n$, and dividing by -1 gives you $n = 24$. But wait! That's not the answer: n is the numerator, but the problem asks for the denominator. So plug 24 into $2n-12$: $2(24)-12 = 36$. And, of course,

$$\frac{2}{3} = \frac{24}{36}$$

18. **8.** Although you may be able to get the answer by trial and error, this problem is really begging to be factored. To factor a *quadratic equation* (that is, an equation with something "squared" in it), you must first set the equation equal to 0. Making the squared term negative is never a good idea, so you should solve as follows. Start with the equation: $p^2 = 3p + 40$. And set everything equal to 0: $p^2 - 3p - 40 = 0$. This equation factors out to $(p-8)(p+5) = 0$. It has two solutions: $p = 8$ and $p = -5$. Because $p > 0$, $p = 8$.

19. **31.** This problem is an example of an alternating sequence; it alternates between adding 4 and subtracting 1 from each term. You could just follow the pattern out to the 21st term, but there's an easier way. Look at all the odd terms: 1, 4, 7, 10. Each term is 3 more than the previous term. So the 21st term must follow this pattern. You can solve this problem by making a list of only the odd terms, like this:

1st	3rd	5th	7th	9th	11th	13th	15th	17th	19th	21st
1	4	7	10	13	16	19	22	25	28	31

20. **30.** This question is all about working with fractions. Consider the following:

$$\frac{1}{x} + \frac{1}{y} = \frac{1}{4}$$

When you're working with fractions, getting a common denominator on each side is a good idea. Here's how it works out:

$$\left(\frac{y}{y}\right)\frac{1}{x} + \left(\frac{x}{x}\right)\frac{1}{y} = \frac{1}{4}$$

$$\frac{y}{xy} + \frac{x}{xy} = \frac{1}{4}$$

$$\frac{x+y}{xy} = \frac{1}{4}$$

Notice how letters are put in alphabetical order; that's standard practice in algebra. Does anything about the fraction on the left side look familiar? It should: The numerator is $x+y$, which is what you're looking for; the denominator is xy, which equals 120. Now you can write $\frac{x+y}{120} = \frac{1}{4}$, so $4(x+y) = 120$, and $x+y = 30$.

Answer Key

Section 1: Reading

1. C	19. D	37. C
2. A	20. C	38. B
3. D	21. D	39. C
4. C	22. A	40. D
5. B	23. D	41. C
6. D	24. C	42. B
7. A	25. C	43. D
8. B	26. D	44. B
9. D	27. B	45. A
10. C	28. C	46. A
11. B	29. A	47. C
12. A	30. C	48. C
13. C	31. D	49. B
14. C	32. B	50. D
15. D	33. C	51. C
16. B	34. D	52. B
17. A	35. A	
18. C	36. B	

Section 2: Writing and Language

1. C	9. D	17. B
2. B	10. B	18. B
3. A	11. D	19. D
4. D	12. B	20. C
5. C	13. B	21. A
6. C	14. C	22. C
7. B	15. D	23. C
8. A	16. A	24. C

25. D	32. C	39. A
26. B	33. D	40. B
27. C	34. D	41. D
28. C	35. B	42. C
29. D	36. C	43. B
30. A	37. D	44. C
31. B	38. B	

Section 3: Math
Calculator section

1. C	14. B	27. A
2. D	15. A	28. A
3. D	16. C	29. D
4. C	17. A	30. B
5. C	18. B	31. **5**
6. B	19. C	32. **70**
7. D	20. B	33. **1.2 or 6/5**
8. D	21. D	34. **17**
9. C	22. A	35. **1/2 or 0.5**
10. C	23. D	36. **6**
11. C	24. C	37. **2,000**
12. D	25. A	
13. B	26. D	

No-calculator section

1. D	8. D	15. D
2. B	9. A	16. **210**
3. B	10. D	17. **36**
4. B	11. C	18. **8**
5. A	12. D	19. **31**
6. A	13. D	20. **30**
7. D	14. C	

Appendix

Scoring Tables for SAT Practice Exams

∙∙

hree hours of work, and you're still not finished! After you take each practice test, if you want to calculate your scores, just follow the steps and use the handy scoring tables provided here.

The scoring of the new SAT is a work in progress, as the College Board refines the exam. Check www.dummies.com/go/sat for the latest updates.

Converting Your Score

Use the following tables to convert the number of answers you got right in each section of the SAT to your overall score.

1. **Check your responses with the answers in Chapter 7.**

   Don't skimp on time here. Read the explanations for each incorrect answer (if you had any!) and figure out what went wrong.

2. **Add up the number of correct answers for the Reading, Writing and Language, and Math sections.**

   Keep these numbers separate.

   Note that Question 37 of the Math Calculator section (the last question of that section) is worth 4 points, while every other question is worth 1 point. No partial credit is given for Question 37.

3. **Convert your scores, using the tables in this appendix.**

   The following tables give you an idea of how you did in the traditional 200 to 800 score format for the exam's three categories: (1) Reading, (2) Writing and Language, and (3) Mathematics.

4. **Add the number of correct answers in the Reading section to the number of correct answers in the Writing and Language section.**

   Exclude the essay. This number represents your work in two major verbal areas.

5. **Convert the total number of Reading and Writing and Language correct answers.**

   Now you have a number between 200 and 800 for the verbal portion of the test.

6. **Add the converted Math score to the converted Reading and Writing and Language score.**

   Your result, which will range from 400 to 1600, is your Composite Score.

7. **If you wrote the essay, score it.**

   Your essay should have three scores, each from 1 to 4: Reading (whether you understood the passage), Analysis (how well you picked apart the arguments and writing style of the passage), and Writing (your own ability to express your thoughts). Each essay is a little different, so a general set of instructions doesn't apply. Chapter 7 provides specific guidelines for the essay question you worked on. Read those guidelines carefully. Chapter 3 provides a sample essay question and detailed scoring guide, if you'd like more help in evaluating your response.

8. Fill in the Score Report at the end of this appendix.

Now you know your strengths and weaknesses. Resolve to work on any problem areas, so your next attempt at the SAT will result in a higher score.

The College Board has stated that it will keep working on the redesigned SAT and its scores, even after the new exam debuts in March 2016. Check www.dummies.com/go/sat for up-to-date scoring changes as they occur.

Table A-1	Reading
Number of Right Answers	**Converted Score**
49 or above	800
48	790
47	780
46	760
45	750
44	740
43	720
42	710
41	700
40	690
39	670
38	660
37	650
36	630
35	620
34	610
33	600
32	580
31	570
30	560
29	540
28	530
27	520
26	510
25	490
24	480
23	470
22	450
21	440
20	430

Number of Right Answers	Converted Score
19	410
18	400
17	390
16	380
15	360
14	350
13	340
12	320
11	310
10	300
9	290
8	270
7	260
6	250
5	230
4	210
3 or below	200

Table A-2	Writing and Language (Multiple-Choice Questions)
Number of Right Answers	**Converted Score**
44	800
43	790
42	770
41	750
40	740
39	730
38	720
37	710
36	700
35	690
34	670
33	660
32	650
31	640
30	630
29	600
28	580
27	560
26	540

(continued)

Table A-2 *(continued)*

Number of Right Answers	Converted Score
25	520
24	500
23	480
22	470
21	450
20	430
19	410
18	390
17	370
16	360
15	350
14	340
13	320
12	300
11	290
10	270
9	260
8	250
7	240
6	230
5	220
4	210
3 or below	200

Table A-3   Combined Reading and Writing and Language Scores

Number of Right Answers on the Reading and the Writing and Language Sections	Converted Score
94 or above	800
91–93	790
88–90	780
86–87	770
84–85	760
82–83	740
80–81	730
79	720
78	710
77	700

Number of Right Answers on the Reading and the Writing and Language Sections	Converted Score
76	690
75	680
74	670
70–73	660
67–69	650
65–66	640
62–64	630
59–61	620
58	610
57	620
56	630
55	620
54	610
53	600
52	590
51	580
50	570
49	560
48	550
47	540
46	530
45	520
44	510
43	500
42	490
41	480
40	470
39	460
38	450
37	440
36	430
35	420
34	410
33	400
32	390
31	380
30	370
29	360
28	350

(continued)

Table A-3 *(continued)*

Number of Right Answers on the Reading and the Writing and Language Sections	Converted Score
27	340
26	330
25	320
24	310
23	300
21–22	290
19–20	270
17–18	260
15–16	250
12–14	240
9–11	230
7–8	220
6	210
5 or below	200

Table A-4 — Essay

Reading	Analysis	Writing

Note: Follow the guidelines in Chapter 7 to score your essay. Insert the numbers in each column.

Table A-5 — Mathematics

Number of Right Answers*	Converted Score
60	800
59	790
58	780
57	770
56	760
55	750
54	740
53	730
52	720
51	710
50	700
49	690
48	680
47	670

Number of Right Answers*	Converted Score
46	660
45	650
44	640
43	630
42	620
41	610
40	600
39	590
38	580
37	570
36	560
35	550
34	540
33	530
32	520
31	510
30	500
29	490
28	480
27	470
26	460
25	450
24	440
23	430
22	420
21	410
20	400
19	390
18	380
17	370
16	360
15	350
14	340
13	330
12	320
11	310
10	300
9	290
8	280
7	270

(continued)

Table A-5 *(continued)*

Number of Right Answers*	Converted Score
6	260
5	250
4	240
3	230
2	220
1	210
0	200

*Question 37 of the Math Calculator section is worth 4 points.

Recording Your Final Scores

For each test, fill in this form.

Converted Reading Score _____ (200–800)

Converted Writing and Language Score _____ (200–800)

Converted Reading and Writing and Language Score _____ (200–800)

Converted Mathematics Score _____ (200–800)

Composite Score _____ (400–1600)

Essay:

Reading _____ (1–4)

Analysis _____ (1–4)

Writing _____ (1–4)

Index

Notes

Notes

Notes

Notes

About the Author

Geraldine Woods has prepared students for the SAT, both academically and emotionally, for the past four decades. She is the author of more than 50 books, including *English Grammar For Dummies, English Grammar Workbook For Dummies, 1,001 Grammar Practice Questions For Dummies,* and earlier editions of *SAT For Dummies,* all published by Wiley. She blogs on grammar at www.grammarianinthecity.com.

Ron Woldoff completed his dual master's degrees at Arizona State University and San Diego State University, where he studied the culmination of business and technology. After several years as a corporate consultant, Ron opened his own company, National Test Prep, where he helps students reach their goals on the GMAT, GRE, SAT, and ACT. He created the programs and curricula for these tests from scratch, using his own observations of the tests and feedback from students. Ron has also taught his own GMAT and GRE programs as an adjunct instructor at both Northern Arizona University and the internationally acclaimed Thunderbird School of Global Management. Ron lives in Phoenix, Arizona, with his lovely wife, Leisah, and their three amazing boys, Zachary, Jadon, and Adam. You can find Ron on the web at testprepaz.com.

Dedication

This book is humbly dedicated to the thousands of students whom we have helped reach their goals. You have taught us as much as we have taught you.

Authors' Acknowledgments

Geraldine Woods: I'd like to thank Peter Bonfanti and Kristin Josephson, whose earlier work on SAT math has been enormously helpful. I appreciate the efforts of Carmen Krikorian, Erin Calligan Mooney, and Sophia Seidner — professionals who never let me down.

Ron Woldoff: I would like to thank my friend Elleyne Kase, who first connected me with the *For Dummies* folks and helped make this book happen. I would also like to thank my friends Ken Krueger, Lionel Hummel, and Jaime Abromovitz, who helped me get things started when I had this wild notion of helping people prepare for standardized college-admissions tests. And more than anyone else, I would like to thank my wife, Leisah, for her continuing support and for always being there for me.

Publisher's Acknowledgments

Acquisitions Editor: Erin Calligan Mooney

Editorial Project Manager: Carmen Krikorian

Development Editor: Christina Guthrie

Copy Editor: Jennette ElNaggar

Technical Editors: Cindy Kaplan, Suzanne Langebartels

Project Coordinator: Sheree Montgomery

Cover Photos: ©iStock.com/Media Mates Oy

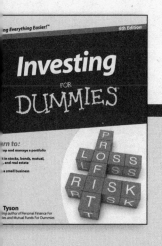

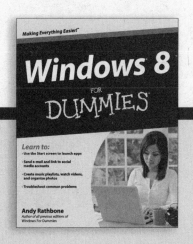

Take Dummies with you everywhere you go!

Whether you are excited about e-books, want more from the web, must have your mobile apps, or are swept up in social media, Dummies makes everything easier.

Leverage the Power

For Dummies is the global leader in the reference category and one of the most trusted and highly regarded brands in the world. No longer just focused on books, customers now have access to the For Dummies content they need in the format they want. Let us help you develop a solution that will fit your brand and help you connect with your customers.

Advertising & Sponsorships

Connect with an engaged audience on a powerful multimedia site, and position your message alongside expert how-to content.

Targeted ads • Video • Email marketing • Microsites • Sweepstakes sponsorship

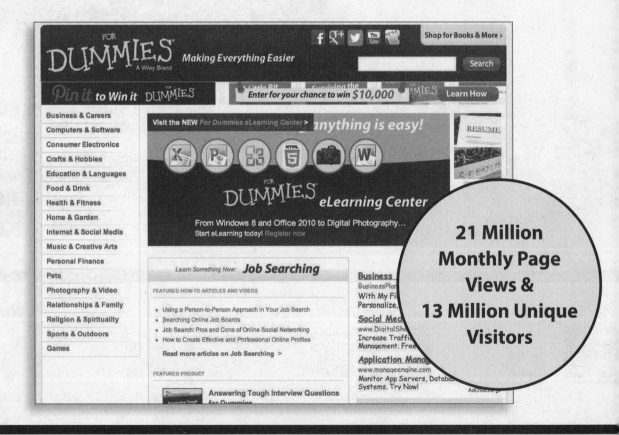

21 Million Monthly Page Views & 13 Million Unique Visitors

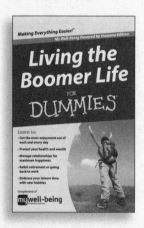